Coach ydia's

No-nonsense Guide to Getting...

off your butt

out of your rut

on with your life

Lydia Martinez
Bonnie Church

ISBN 9781890052461

Library of Congress Control Number: 2011927634

Copyright ©2011 - Lydia Martinez

Published by: Shut Up and Listen Publishing
Web Site: www.lydiamartinez.com

Book Design: Terry Henry
Illustrations: Andy Rogers
Cover Photography: John Middlebrook

Printed in Korea through Four Colour Print Group

Dedicated to:

Children - born without a silver spoon in your mouth .

You, who, despite the lack of wealth, connection or societys' blessing, chose to succeed anyway.

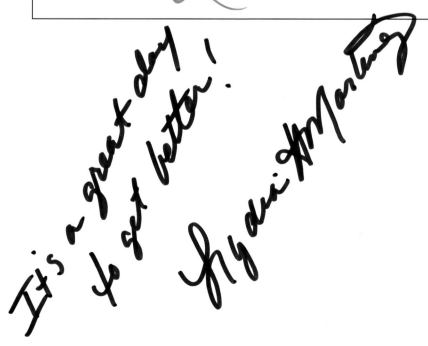

CONTENTS

ACKNOWLEDGEMENTS

Though this book is about things I have learned in life, I feel like my journey has just begun. In order to accomplish anything in life, you need people around you who believe in you and push you to be the best you can be. You need friends who will set you straight and keep you grounded. You need role models who will instill the belief that what you dream is possible. Many have touched my life professionally and personally. Special heartfelt thanks to:

Bonnie Church, my Co-author Bonnie, you absolutely AMAZE me. You are gifted, intuitive and encouraging. You saw in me a story worth sharing and helped me birth this book. You brought clarity to my deepest thoughts and wrapped just the right words around them. Your friendship and your creative partnership mean a lot.

Billy Izer There are people that come into your life just at the right time and when they do you know that your life will be changed forever. You are definitely that one. In the midst of our personal craziness you never stopped believing in me. Your belief in me catalyzed my belief in myself. You pushed me toward me dreams [For the record: sometimes really ticking me off!]. You supported me in every goal I have set and every project I have undertaken. Thank you, Billy!!

Bonnie Gallagher You have always been there for me and helped me in more ways than you will ever know.

Kelly and Vicki Whited You are two of the most loyal people I know. Thank you for laughing, and crying with me. Thank you for sharing your wisdom and most of all, for being my friends.

Andy Webb You are an incredible role model. You keep your heart and priorities in the right place. I have learned a lot from you.

Dr. Nancy Miller –Ihli Gosh, You're smart. Thanks for being you. No doubt about it, if I had you as a teacher, I definitely would have been a scientist. You've taught me so much.

Shannon Wallace Jr. Thanks for taking me from good shape to awesome shape, being a friend and sharing your story. I know doing that type of thing is tough on lugs like us.

Dennis Franks (Coach D) Thank you for giving me the chance to prove myself. You always knew there was heart and talent wrapped in that rough exterior. You always reminded me, "Don't get too comfortable— you're only as good as your last game." Oh, by the way, "You won the game, but not by a hundred points."

Loren and JR Ridinger Thank you for teaching me to "Dream Big - You will never be bigger than your Dreams." Thank you for Market America – an incredible vehicle to help others earn what they deserve to earn and get them where they want to go.

To my sister, Maria A toast once heard: "To my big sister, who never found her second Easter egg until I'd found my first." ~ Robert Brault

To my brothers You agitated, you picked on me and you made me tough. I love my big brothers. HOWEVER, I'm still annoyed that you nicknamed me 'Bubbles' after Michael Jackson's monkey. Worse yet, you still call me that.

To my Mom People didn't always understand why I would often have two sandwiches in my lunch bag. I knew. I knew it was for my friend who often came to school with no food. You taught me strength and true compassion.

Coach Lydia and Bonnie Church would both like to acknowledge the following.

Our gifted creative production team

Terry Henry of (abundant1.com)   Your keen sense of design and creative direction for this project was vital to its success. You made our original idea, so much more beautiful. You rock!

John Middlebrook of (Mid-Maryland Photography)   We appreciate the pains you took to get just the right shot. You are a true artist.

Andy Rogers of (andyrogersdesign.com)   Your original artwork nailed it.

Olivia Vallecillo, proof-reading, copy-editing   Thank you for looking over our shoulders and reminding us to dot our i's and cross our t's.

Those of you who bring us hope and inspiration through your story
Tamara Adell – Wellness coach and overcomer
Michele Cooper – Writer, musician, Champion Figure skater
Michelle Hepfler – Wellness coach, entrepreneur
Beverly Pinske – Author, of Pawns of Deception
Jesse Pipes – Founding Director, of worldcampforkids.org
Shannon Wallace, Jr. – Founder and owner, of 368 Athletics

Those of you who provided encouragement and insight
Alice Grimsley – Bonnie's mom and mentor
Michael Church – Bonnie's wise and loving husband of 36 years
Meredith Church - Bonnie's sounding board [and daughter]
Joy Clary Brown –Author, of The Creation Diet: Gods pattern for health, happiness and holiness
Sherrie Norris – Editor, All About Women Magazine
Dr. Tracy Parrish, MD – A doctor with a heart!
Dr. Marilyn Carter, MD –Hippocrates would be proud!
Michele Townsend, RPh – A pharmacist who knows the healing power of food.

A word from Co-author, Bonnie Church

Lydia and I seem as different as night and day. I am a baby boomer; Lydia a Generation X'er. I am married; she is not. I am both a mom and grandma; she is the quintessential career woman. I love the seclusion of my home in the Blue Ridge Mountains; she loves urban energy and opportunity. But, beneath the surface of our differences, we have much in common.

Our common experience is what attracted us to collaborate on this project. Lydia and I were both raised in large, 'working poor' families. We had beloved, mentally ill fathers and resourceful, strong mothers. Our destructive adolescent choices were different, but sprang from a similar pain. We understand how easy it is to get stuck in the pain of the past, or disoriented by the confusion of the present.

The lessons we've learned along the way guided the development of this book. I have been involved with writing projects with other authors. This collaboration was different. It was more like writing down conversations shared with a sister, rather than hammering out text for a book.

From our conversations, this book of steps was born; steps to get you from where you are, to where you want to go. Each step is framed by wisdom that existed long before either author was born - time tested principles such as:

- Love yourself.
- Love your neighbor as much as you love yourself.
- Be humble – your time, your talent and your body are gifts that have been given.
- Be grateful – your time, your talent and your body are gifts that have been given.
- Demonstrate your love for God, the giver, by using these gifts wisely.

It is our hope and expectation that this guide will help you create the energy you need to break the bad habits that stumble you and live the life that inspires you.

Bonnie Church
Co-author, columnist, Certified life and wellness coach

For more inspiration on how to 'get on with your life', visit Lydia and Bonnies' life-coaching blog at www.alifenow.com

PART **1**

Lydia's Story

There is a saying. You can't judge a book by the cover. You've seen the cover of this book. You see a woman fit, smiling and energetic. No denying it, that woman is me. But what you don't see is the little girl at the core of the woman on the cover. That little girl is just as real. Let me tell you about her.

Every little girl wants to be loved by her dad and I was no different. My dad was handsome, funny and a magician of sorts. He didn't do his tricks on stage in front of thousands; he performed in our living room for me and my siblings. I was the baby of the family. I believed every trick, I laughed at every joke. I savored every illusion.

Those were the good days. Sadly, there were even more bad days; Days when dad was angry, violent, loud and scary; Days when you knew you had to 'watch your step' so that you did not tip him into one of his moods. My dad was mentally ill. He had highs and he had lows.

Children of mentally ill parents have some unique struggles. Basic needs are unmet. Mentally ill parents often do not make good providers. We were fortunate that my dad worked consistently, but due to his insecurities and cultural background he would not let mom work. There were a lot of kids in the family to support. We struggled financially.

In a healthy home, the unique gifts of each child are observed and cultivated. In a home with a mentally ill parent, there is no energy to focus on the kids. The focus is on accommodating the needs and moods of the mentally ill parent.

The children of mentally ill parents often endure criticism, insults and physical violence disguised as discipline. The psychological damage often takes years to undo, and may last a lifetime.

Very often these children suffer in silence. Mental illness is the family secret that must be kept. You just can't go out and discuss it with anyone.

My mom was resilient and resourceful. She did the best she could to provide stability and guidance for us. Sadly, she was often the lightning rod for Dad's rage. There were many days when I would awaken to the sounds of violence, furniture being thrown and mom being beaten and screamed at. One day dad hit mom so hard, I could hear her ribs crack.

I was the baby girl. I often escaped the worst of his rage. My brothers were not so fortunate. Dad would berate, push them around and beat them.

My ability to trust was seriously damaged by the time that I was school age. It was further damaged when at 8 years old I was molested. There seemed to be no safe place for me in the world.

Home was scary, but the neighborhood had its challenges too. Dad was Mexican-American. Mom was American. We were half-Mexican, and we looked it. Kids can be cruel. They would hurl racist barbs at me and my siblings – wet back, half breed, greasy Mexican. You know the saying, 'sticks and stones can break my bones, but words will never hurt me'? Trust me, it's not true.

Some kids find refuge at school. Not I. School was a painful place. I had a curious mind and strong verbal communication skills, but reading was a challenge. If you can't read well, you will fall behind in every subject. My struggle with academics compounded my insecurities. Frustrated with trying, at 16, I quit school.

By the time I hit adolescence the voices in my head were loud, "You will never be good enough! You will never be smart enough! You will never amount to anything!"

No matter how many people told me I was smart, I felt stupid. No matter how many people told me I was pretty, I felt ugly. When I looked in the mirror, I saw a girl with the wrong skin color, the wrong shape nose and even the wrong last name. Martinez – it sounded too Mexican. It labeled me as inferior to the rest of my friends.

If anyone attempted to compliment me, I assumed they were lying. They were just trying to get something from me. Sarcasm and toughness became my protective armor. Don't even try to get close to me.

The negative voices in my head became harsh task masters, driving me into unhealthy behaviors. I became obsessed with looking like the 'beautiful people'. I figured with an extreme diet I could look like those air-brushed models on television. I became a diet fad junkie, on a quest to find the next best fat-buster. The results were predictable. I felt tired, grouchy, unfocussed. I was yo-yoing between thin and unfit and chunky and unfit. Despite my determination, I eventually ended up 30 lbs. over my ideal weight.

I sought the company of people as insecure and self-destructive as I was. I discovered I could numb my pain with alcohol. I became a regular in the party crowd. I fit right in. I could drink and tell funny stories with the best of them. Fortunately, despite my poor choices, I did not get enslaved by alcoholism or drug addiction.

I was hustler. I got my first job waiting tables at age 14. I was too young to be put on the payroll, so they paid me under the table. I always had a job, and I always worked hard. As I upgraded my image with clothes, cars and things, people were no longer looking at me as the

Mexican girl, who struggled in school and lived in a crazy family. I was getting a lot of attention for being attractive, funny and clever.

But as parties do, mine ended. One day, I got a call from mom. She was frantic. She told me to get to the hospital right way. Dad had a heart attack. He died before I got there.

3 days later, I watched as my brothers, tears streaming down their faces, carried Dads' coffin to his grave. It was over. I was left with many regrets. I never got to tell my dad I loved him. I never got to tell him he was forgiven. I wasn't even sure if he ever loved me.

My hard work earned me a decent income, but I did not manage it wisely. By the age of 28, I had run my life and my bank account into the ground. I was completely broke – homeless and carless, sitting on a curb with a garbage bag full of clothes and my dog, Buddie, by my side. I had gone from being pretty, fun-loving and prosperous to beat down, tired and out of shape.

That hard cold curb was a blessing. It was there I had an 'AHA' moment. It was there that it hit me that what I was doing was not working. It was there that I made the decision to get off my butt, out of my rut and on with my life.

The journey from that hard, cold curb to the life I lead now has not been easy. I had to go through the process of reflecting on the pain of the past so that I could move on. I had to learn forgiveness and acceptance of others and of myself. I had to define my goals and chart out my steps.

I'm now 40. I feel better about myself than I have ever felt. I eventually earned my high school diploma and several fitness and life coaching certifications. I am more fit than I have ever been. I have trimmed off 30 lbs. and am now doing fitness training with young athletes half my age. I have created multiple income streams and achieved millionaire status with my business. I am more excited about the future than I have ever been. I still have many items on my 'Do Before I Die' list and I plan to do them all.

This no-nonsense guide includes what I have learned along the way. It is a book of action. It offers simple steps that can lead you to where you want to go.

So, now you know my story. Time to write your own.

7 STEPS TO GETTING OFF YOUR BUTT

GET OFF YOUR BUTT

If you want to get on with your life, you have to start with taking care of your body. Let's face it - If your health fails, it will overshadow everything else. If you don't feel well, you will not have the energy, mental focus and self-esteem that you need to envision and create a life of purpose.

Taking care of your body means making healthy choices about what you eat and the way you live. Your choices will determine whether you store fat, or burn it, whether your mind is clear or foggy, whether you feel energetic or sleepy, whether you live long and well or short and sick.

Sad to say, as a nation we are not making the best choices. Diet and lifestyle disease is the most common cause of death in the world. Our poor choices are creating an epidemic of non-contagious and largely preventable diseases – obesity, cancer, Type 2 diabetes, cardio-vascular disease and osteoporosis.

I have seen the devastation of these bad choices up close. My father died of a Type 2 diabetes-related heart attack at age 58. I have grandparents who were consumed by cancer. I have cried with kids who were suffering the stigma and pain of obesity. I have heard the anxiety in the voices of my clients who have been told by their doctors, "If you don't change your ways, you are going to die young."

Yes, what we choose to eat, and how we choose to live affects us dramatically. The good news - it is never too late to choose wisely.

I have also seen the dramatic turn around that comes when a client begins to make better choices. Those same kids I wept with; I have also celebrated with. I have seen their self-image and life goals change as they become fit. I have heard the testimonials of hundreds of people transformed from sick and tired, to healthy and energetic.

Yes, simple choices can produce dramatic results.

GET OFF YOUR BUTT outlines the simple choices you need to make if you want to lead a healthy life. Everything written here is derived from my work with hundreds of individuals. It is based on countless hours of health and fitness certification training. It is my attempt to crystallize the best of all wellness wisdom.

This section is not intended to be an essay on nutritional science. If you want to study things in greater detail, there are countless books and medical journals to pore over. I encourage you to do so if you are so inclined.

The focus of GET OFF YOUR BUTT is to construct a simple action plan for:

- Sustaining your energy throughout the day.

- Sharpening your mental focus.
- Stabilizing your moods.
- Bringing your body to an optimal weight.
- Living the life you were designed to live.

These steps are not something merely to be read, they are things to do. So get ready to take action. Lifestyle change comes one step at a time.

If you need the assistance of a wellness or life coach to keep you on track during the process of change, find one. Consider it an investment in yourself. Consider it one of the most important investments you can make. For additional resources to help you with diet, exercise and lifestyle decisions visit www.lydiamartinez.com.

BUTT STEP ONE:
OUT WITH THE CRAP

Keeping the crap out of your house will help to keep it out of your mouth. Trust me. Eventually 'feeling good again' will taste so much better than all that crap.

To protect yourself from all the toxic crap in the world you would have to live in a bubble. Sadly, there is no way to totally avoid exposure to chemicals in the environment, or the hormones and antibiotics in products like meat and milk. Nonetheless, it is important to do all you can to limit your exposure. You will never get 'off your butt' unless you do. Toxic overload creates hormonal imbalances that make you feel lethargic, unfocused and moody. If you are overweight, it is worse. Toxins lodge in fat cells. So the fatter you are, the more toxic you will be.

To lend your body a hand in keeping the toxin levels down;

- Filter your water
- Eat Organic
- Wash your veggies and fruits

My main concern is the deadly stuff that you are forking into your mouth on a daily basis. I call it crap. If you are really serious about feeling energetic, focused and stable, you need to get it out of your life.

Grab a trash bag and let's go to the kitchen.

Toss the bitter sweets

Sugar is not bad in itself. It is actually the main fuel of the body. You need it to keep you alert and alive. What makes sugar good or bad is how much you eat and how it is packaged.

When sugar is 'packaged' in veggies, small amounts are released slowly as the fiber in the veggies breaks down. The problems begin when the sugar-source is stripped of its fiber, and eaten in excess. This sudden jolt of the sweet stuff triggers metabolic madness.

It looks like this:

- It is mid-morning and you are at your desk at work.
- Your stomach is growling and you begin to crave a snack.
- You go to the vending machine and buy a package of 6 small cookies.
- You planned to just eat one, but, guess what, back at your desk, you mindlessly inhale the entire pack.

Congratulations! You just ate 6 teaspoons of sugar masquerading as a ball of sweet lard flanked by 2 pieces of chocolate cardboard. As you scour the empty package with a wet index finger to make sure you get every last crumb, there is a crisis brewing inside your body.

All that sugar has alerted your pancreas [a banana shaped broom closet] to bring out insulin [the hormonal broom]. Insulin is commissioned to sweep that sugar out of your blood and into your cells. It will sweep a small amount into your liver, a small amount into your muscle and the rest will get swept into fat cells.

As the sugar gets packed away, your blood sugar begins to drop. Your body knows that if it drops too low you are in trouble. To prevent a rapid drop, your adrenals release cortisol. Cortisol causes you to crave more sugar, and store it as fat. These cravings drive you back to the vending machine and the cycle continues.

**GRAB A TRASH BAG
AND TOSS THE CRAP**

- Blood sugar up
- Blood sugar down
- Sugar stored as fat
- Cravings awakened
- Eat more sugar
- Blood sugar up
- Blood sugar down
- Sugar stored as fat
- Cravings awakened

You get the point.

Excess sugar creates problems, so why not toss it, to prevent temptation?

I am not just talking about the white stuff. Sugar is disguised by other names. Some of those names sound 'down right good for ya. 'High fructose corn syrup' [hfcs] is one of those names. High fructose corn syrup is actually a high octane sugar made from corn. It is cheap to produce and easy to disguise. It is slipped into everything from ketchup to canned fruit.

This deadly syrup messes with the hormones that control your appetite. This means you are likely to crave increasing amounts of the sweet stuff. The more you eat, the more intense the peaks and valleys of the blood sugar roller coaster. Over time, this vicious cycle can lead to chronic diseases: Type 2 diabetes, heart disease and cancer to name a few.

My advice - Bust the sugar before it busts you. Get the trash bag and toss the following:

- Bags of Sugar – white, raw, turbinado
- Anything with corn syrup on the label
- Boxed foods with added sugars

Toss the bleached grains, crushed beyond recognition

I have a question for you. If you went to the bank with a $100 bill, and asked for change and the teller gave you $3.00 back would you consider yourself ENRICHED by the transaction, or DEFRAUDED? Well, that basically describes what is done to supposedly 'ENRICHED' flour products. Most of the good stuff is stripped out – the bran and the germ that contain the fiber, vitamins and minerals. You are left with white powder and a few vitamins sprinkled in. Perhaps a better description would be 'DEFRAUDED' flour.

Why would food manufacturers go to all the trouble to turn real food into a phantom food? Because, refining the grains extends the shelf life of the product and makes it easier to cook. The problem is this – refined grains turn into sugar rapidly – causing your blood sugar to skyrocket. And you know, by now, how bad that is.

So, let's get the trash bag and toss those tortillas, pasta and bread products that contain refined grains. [If the label does not say whole grain, it goes].

Toss the sizzled and chemically altered fats

There are good fats and there are bad fats. The bad ones are those that have been chemically changed through over-heating [trans-fat] or blasted with hydrogen [partially hydrogenated fats].

These altered fats, alter your health for the worse. They can increase "bad" cholesterol [LDL] - the kind that gums up your arteries. They can decrease the good cholesterol [HDL]- the kind that cleans up your arteries and they can raise triglycerides [blood-fat].

If you were swimming around in your arteries you would see the damage the bad fats do. When you eat these toxic fats, the arteries constrict [you want them dilated so blood can flow smoothly]. The walls of the arteries become sticky like Velcro™ [you want them smooth like Teflon™]. Your blood becomes sticky and more likely to clot. In other words, you are a heart attack waiting to happen.

These bad fats [specifically the over-heated trans fats] also create inflammation in your body. You are familiar with the inflammation that is red, swollen and painful. There is another kind of inflammation raging in your body that is at the root of heart disease, diabetes, cancer, asthma, inflammatory bowel disease and Alzheimer's disease.

I know, throwing out these destructive, but 'Oh, so tasty,' foods is painful, but eating them is even more painful. So, toss 'em!

Toss the factory food

We are a busy people. We don't have time to cook, let alone go to the market each day. We have stuff to do. It is convenient to buy foods already prepared for us – foods in a box or wrapped in plastic sleeves.

The body does not recognize processed food as real food, because it is not. Processed food is manufactured - in a factory. Those little sleeves of 'cheese food' you melt on your burger have more in common with the square plastic envelopes they are stored in than with your body. You might be better off eating a high-quality dog kibble.

Those little sleeves of 'cheese food' you melt on your burger have more in common with the square plastic envelopes they are stored in than with your body. You might be better off eating a high-quality dog kibble.

Get the trash bag. If it is processed beyond recognition, with unpronounceable names on the label, toss it.

Toss the nutrient-leeched, dried stuff

When cooked beyond recognition, soaked in preservatives and enhanced with sugar and salt even the good food is not very nutritious.

For example, canned veggies and fruits might have as much as 90% of their nutritional value leached through a high-heat canning process. It is also quite common for salt and sugar to be added for flavor.

Dried fruits can have twice the calories and they spike sugar more rapidly than fresh fruit. They are easily over-eaten because they are smaller and don't contain water. Many of the vitamins are depleted during the heating process, including vitamin C. Unless organic, they are treated with sulfur dioxide as a color fixative, a chemical thought to trigger asthma.

Bottom line: Out with the cans and dried foods, in with the fresh fruits and veggies.

Toss the diet drinks

Even one "diet" drink per day can increase the likelihood of gaining weight by as much as 60%. Why? Artificial sweeteners trigger something called the "cephalic phase insulin response". In other words, your body is tricked into thinking the blood sugar has elevated and releases insulin as though you ate real sugar. This leads to that malicious metabolic cycle of sugar cravings and fat storage.

If you are really serious about getting the crap out, you will toss this too.

Toss the excess alcohol

A macho, muscly guy swaggers into the bar, orders a whisky, swigs it down. "Ahhh, what a man!" Or, so he thinks. Little does he know, he just increased his levels of the feminine hormone – estrogen.

Yes, excess alcohol releases estrogen into your blood stream. When exposed to estrogen the body will store fat and decrease muscle. Think 'BEER BELLY.' When you drink alcohol, your body makes it a priority to deal with the alcohol and it will put some of the other processes on hold, including fat-burning. Just 2 alcoholic beverages can cut your fat burning mojo by 73% - right when you need it most! Alcohol also increases your appetite for buffalo wings, cold pizza, nachos, you name it. When you are buzzed, you will probably eat it.

Most dangerous of all, excess alcohol diminishes coordination and reasoning. That is why it is illegal to drive 'under the influence.' To top it off, there is a good chance you will not sleep well. And some of you know from experience what it feels like to wake up the next morning with a 'hang over.'

With alcohol, a little goes a long way. So, if your refrigerator is stocked with more sixers than food, get the trash bag. You need to thin it out a bit.

Toss the excess caffeine

This is a painful subject for me. I like my daily dose of Starbucks. But the truth is, if you need a jolt of Joe to get your day going, something is wrong. Caffeine boosts energy by stimulating the central nervous system and increasing the heart rate and blood pressure. A little bit might make you feel jazzed and ready to roll, but too much and you will end up jittery and anxious.

One serious side effect - an excess of caffeine can sabotage your sleep. That sets up a bad pattern:

- Use caffeine
- Sleep poorly
- Wake up tired
- Use caffeine to wake up
- Sleep poorly

Whether your 'fix' comes from an espresso machine, a teapot, or a vending machine, it's still 'a fix.' Caffeine is addictive. The slump you feel when its effects wear off compels you to consume more -- turning it into a crutch.

Bottom line is- you need to reduce your intake of caffeine and drink more water.

Toss in a bit of grace

There you stand with a tear in your eye and a box of cream puffs in your hand. With a quiver in your voice you ask, "You mean, I can never eat my lard and sugar stuffed favorite junk food again?"

Good news! There is grace in the journey. As long as this bad stuff is not the centerpiece of your life, you can enjoy it occasionally. But, it's better to enjoy crap away from the house. Keeping the crap out of your house will help to keep it out of your mouth. Trust me. Eventually 'feeling good again' will taste so much better than all that crap.

Do the kitchen cupboards look a bit empty? Time to go to the grocery store and pick up some real food.

BUTT STEP TWO:
IN WITH THE GOOD STUFF

If you are doing it right, the fat will burn, the mind will clear
and the moods will stabilize. Best of all, you won't be
walking around with ravenous cravings
clawing at your willpower.

If you are being treated for a medical condition or are under the care of a physician, discuss all diets and lifestyle changes with your doctor.

You trashed the crap [or almost, right?]. Now it's time to put the good food in. Out with the crap, in with the good stuff pretty much sums up a healthy diet.

The 'Off Your Butt' nutritional plan requires a daily rhythm of:

- mindfully eating good food
- faithfully drinking pure water and healing teas
- sensibly supplementing to fill in the gaps

If you are doing it right, the fat will burn, the mind will clear and the moods will stabilize. Best of all, you won't be walking around with ravenous cravings clawing at your willpower.

The 'Off Your Butt' Kitchen will include:

- Fresh Food from all 3 food groups [organic when possible]
- Seasonings
- Water filtration
- High-quality supplements

CHOOSE FOODS FROM ALL 3 FOOD GROUPS

Carbohydrates [aka Carbs]

Carbohydrates provide the energy you need to be alert and energetic. When you eat a carb, it breaks down into 'sugar' [a.k.a. blood glucose]. Blood glucose is to the body, what gas is to a car. You can't run on 'empty'. The foods in the carb group include everything from table sugar to tomatoes; from sticky white rice to chewy whole grains.

Just like fragrances, there are a lot of variations. Both a skunk and a perfume give off an odor; but if you want to enhance a romantic evening, I would suggest the benefits of a perfume. It's the same with carbs. Some are really bad for you, and some are really good.

Among other things, one thing that makes a carb bad or good is how quickly it breaks down into sugar. Slower is better. Fiber is the braking system for carbohydrates. Fiber slows down the release of sugar from the carbs you eat. When the sugar is slowly released the body can use it for immediate needs rather than storing it as fat. Fiber also helps to bulk your poop, scrub out the digestive track and make elimination of wastes more efficient.

The rate at which a carb breaks down into sugar is called the glycemic index. High glycemic index carbs [high GI] break down fast. Low glycemic index [low GI] carbs, break down slowly, and moderate glycemic index carbs are somewhere in between.

THE CARB KEY: The difference between the good carb [low GI] and the bad [high GI] is fiber. Fresh vegetables, fruits and whole grains are wrapped in fiber. Refined, peeled, processed and overcooked foods are not. That is why we dumped them.

In With The Good Stuff

Protein

Protein is to your body what wood and nails are to your home. It is needed to build and repair every structure in your body. You must supply yourself with fresh protein daily. If you are deficient in protein, it will show up as brittle hair, dull skin, stooped shoulders, flaccid muscles, and a breakdown of every vital organ. Not pretty.

There are animal forms of protein: chicken, fish, lamb, and pork, for example.
There are vegetable forms of protein: beans and some grains.

THE PROTEIN KEY: You want lean and clean. Choose proteins that are not marbled with fat or tainted with antibiotics, hormones and pesticides.

Fats

We need to eat fat-containing foods each day, too. We don't need much, but we need some. Fat is a key ingredient for building hormones. Hormones carry the instructions to each organ and gland to tell it what to do next. Fats help us stay happy, energetic and satisfied with our meals.

Again, not all fats are alike. Good fats burn blubber, clean the arteries, and help you 'feel full'. Bad fats clog the arteries, gum up your blood, and bulk up your body. In sum—Good fats heal the body. Bad fats harm the body.

The best fats come in two types:

Monounsaturated fats [MUFA] These important fats lower bad cholesterol [artery gunk] and raise good cholesterol [artery cleanser]. Research also shows that MUFAs may enhance blood sugar control. You find monounsaturated fat in nuts, avocado and olives.

Polyunsaturated fats [PUFA] These fats lower the bad cholesterol [artery gunk]. This category of fats also includes the very important omega 3 fats. Research has shown omega 3 can have a positive impact on your brain, heart, lungs, eyes, digestion, immune system and, oh yeah, your metabolism. Fatty fish and eggs are an animal source of polyunsaturated fats. Flax and nuts are a plant source.

The worst fats come in two types:

'Always bad' trans-fat The French fries and glazed donut fats. These are the fats that have been altered through excess heat [fried] or chemicals [hydrogenated].

'Sometimes bad' saturated fats You need a little saturated fat, but an excess has been associated with obesity and heart disease, weight gain and arterial gunk. Saturated fats are found in animal products, both dairy and meat.

THE FAT KEY: Eat adequate amounts of fish, nuts, avocado and olives [use olive oil]. Limit the fats from dairy and meat. Eliminate the overheated and chemically treated fats.

DRINK PLENTY OF WATER

To replace the water you spit, urinate and breathe out, a good rule of thumb is to drink 2 quarts of water a day. Those who are exercising, drinking diuretic drinks [coffee, alcohol], or are overweight need more.

Water is a natural appetite suppressant. Lack of water can lead to overeating. When you think you are feeling hungry, your body may in fact be signaling that you are thirsty!

It's part of the body's built-in survival mechanism - to store up the essential nutrients in short supply. So, if you don't drink enough water, you are 'conditioning' your body to store water. And water is bulk and unwanted inches. Many people notice a reduction in weight and inches when they start drinking more water.

Water offers an extensive range of functions essential to life.

- If you don't drink enough water you can't get the full benefit of nutrients in the food you eat. Water distributes and delivers nutrients to the cells.
- Without enough water flowing through your system to carry out wastes and toxins, you would literally drown in your own poisonous, metabolic wastes.

- Water lubricates lung tissue to reduce asthma and other lung related issues.
- Water plumps the skins which slows signs of aging.
- Water reduces constipation.
- Water helps to prevent kidney stones.
- Water supports healthy eyes.
- Water lubricates the joints so you are less stiff and achy.

You get some water from fruits and vegetables. Herbal teas are also an effective way to get some of your water. However, you need some straight and purified water perhaps with a slice of lemon.

> *The 'Off Your Butt' nutritional plan requires a daily rhythm of:*
>
> • *mindfully eating good food*
> • *faithfully drinking pure water and healing teas*
> • *sensibly supplementing to fill in the gaps*

Water should be 'sipped' throughout the day. Just like you don't want to overwhelm your body with too much food at once, you don't want to drown it with too much water at once.

WATER KEY: Drink water that has been filtered to eliminate environmental toxins. Carry your water in glass or stainless steel. Chemicals from plastic containers can leech into the water and contaminate it. These chemicals are estrogenic and have been associated with breast cancer and hormonal imbalances.

SPICE THINGS UP

Spices and herbs not only make your food taste better, but they can support your health.

Sea salt: A little bit of salt goes a long way. Too much can be damaging to your kidneys and heart. When you do use salt; use sea salt. It has less sodium and more trace minerals than refined salt.

Black pepper: Pepper increases the production of hydrochloric acid, thereby improving digestion and reducing flatulence.

Vinegar: Vinegar is a good base for healthy salad dressings. It has been shown to slow down the conversion of starchy foods into glucose, thus minimizing the chances of a spike.

Garlic: Garlic is a natural antibiotic. The body does not appear to build up resistance to garlic, so its positive health benefits continue over time.

Cinnamon: Research chemist, Richard A. Anderson and co-workers at the Beltsville (Maryland) Human Nutrition Research Center found cinnamon made fat cells more responsive to insulin. Remember, insulin is the hormone that regulates the level of glucose in the blood.

Basil: Basil reduces inflammation in the body. Eugenol, a component of basil, blocks the activity of an enzyme in the body called cyclooxygenase (COX). Many non-steroidal, over-the-counter, anti-inflammatory medications (NSAIDS), including aspirin and ibuprofen, as well as the commonly used medicine acetaminophen, work by inhibiting this same enzyme.

Chili peppers: Chili peppers were once thought to cause ulcers. Not only do they not cause ulcers, they potentially help prevent them. Chili peppers stimulate the stomach to secrete protective buffering juices against the bacteria that causes ulcers.

Cumin seeds: Cumin seeds are a very good source of iron. Iron increases hemoglobin - the transport system that gets oxygen from the lungs to all body cells. Iron is also instrumental in keeping the immune system healthy.

Ginger: Ginger helps to eliminate gastrointestinal distress. It also reduces the dizziness, nausea, vomiting and cold sweats of motion sickness.

Oregano: Oregano contains oils which have been shown to inhibit the growth of bacteria.

Sage: Sage is an outstanding memory enhancer. An extract from the root of Chinese sage was found to contain acetylcholinesterase (AChE) inhibitors. The memory loss characteristic of Alzheimer's disease is accompanied by an increase of AChE activity.

Turmeric [curcumin]: Turmeric might prove to be to the spice cabinet powerhouse. Curcumin is potentially cancer protective. It seems to help the body to destroy mutated cancer cells, so they cannot spread and cause more harm. Curcumin also potentially prevents the oxidation of cholesterol in the body. Oxidized cholesterol damages blood vessels and builds up in the plaques that can lead to heart attack or stroke. The most active ingredient in this spice is bisdemethoxycurcumin, which seems to boost the activity of the immune system in Alzheimer's patients, helping to clear the amyloid beta plaques characteristic of the disease.

SEASONING KEY: Stock your spice cabinet with all your favorite flavors. Not only will this make your good food more appealing, but it could potentially increase the health benefits of your meals.

SUPPLEMENT SENSIBILY

Wouldn't it be nice if we were in the Garden of Eden and every bit of food was teeming with nutrients? Well, we're not.

The Standard American Diet [SAD] consists of food that is...

✓ grown in demineralized soil
✓ picked before it is ripened

✓ shipped cross country in gas infused containers to aid in ripening
✓ cooked beyond recognition
✓ disguised with excess sugar and salt

To make up for the deficits in the food we eat, supplementation is helpful.

QUALITY MATTERS

Choose your supplements wisely. Not all supplements are alike.

Your supplement should be:
  • Potent and pure
  • Easily absorbed - What's the use of taking a supplement if your body can't absorb it and the nutrients pass through you and end up in the toilet?

HOW TO ENSURE POTENCY AND PURITY: A reputable company will provide supplements that meet or exceed the requirements for potency and purity set by the FDA. These supplements should be tested by independent labs, not just the manufacturers 'inside' lab. Some examples of supplements that can have 'the right stuff' in a toxic base if you are not careful include:

  • Fish Oil: In my opinion the best source of omega 3 is fish oil. The problem: Fish oil taken from toxic fish can be toxic to us. So, it is important to find an oil derived from small fish, fished out of pure waters, purified through micro-distillation and tested to ensure it is indeed pure.
  • Calcium: Coral was once touted as the ultimate source for calcium. Later, it was discovered that coral calcium can have potentially high lead levels. If you are not dealing with a reputable brand whose manufacturers carefully tested for things like lead, your supplement could be tainted with undesirable ingredients.

HOW TO ENSURE HIGH ABSORPTION: Supplements should be well absorbed. If your body can't absorb it, it can't use it. I prefer isotonic formulations over compressed and glazed tablets. An isotonic formula is the same pH and density as your body fluids. When taken on an empty stomach, research indicates that isotonic products are absorbed more rapidly and at a high concentration. Other formulations can pass through your body with minimal absorption. It doesn't matter what the label promises, if your body can't absorb it, you have wasted your money.

SUPPLEMENTATION KEY: Choose high quality supplements that are both potent and pure and easily absorbed.

LETS GO SHOPPING

A WORD ABOUT ORGANIC:

Whenever I can, I eat organic food. Organic food is food from plants and animals that is produced without the use of synthetic fertilizers, artificial pesticides, herbicides, antibiotics, growth hormones, feed additives or genetically modified organisms (GMOs). Eating organic food limits your exposure to dangerous chemicals that can cause serious harm.

I realize that not all of us can afford to go 100% organic every time we shop. To help you save money, eliminate those foods that contain the heaviest burden of pesticides, additives and hormones. You can reduce your pesticide exposure by as much as 80% if you avoid the most contaminated fruits and vegetables.

The following list contains some of the most toxic foods on the market. This is based on the 2010 statistical analysis conducted by the USDA [U.S. Dept. of Agriculture] and the FDA [Food and Drug Administration].

- Meat, Dairy and Eggs
- Coffee
- Celery
- Strawberries [particularly imported]
- Apples
- Blueberries
- Nectarines
- Bell peppers
- Spinach
- Kale
- Cherries
- White Potatoes
- Grapes [particularly imported]

COACH LYDIAS SHOPPING LIST
'Organic' has been designated for all the foods that are on the 'most toxic' list.

Beans (and other legumes): Beans are one of the richest sources of soluble fiber, which is the key to good blood sugar control. Steady, level blood sugar will help you stay mentally clear, energetic and satisfied with your meal.

Beans have "resistant" starch, which resists being digested. It ferments and rebuilds the intestinal lining. It creates short-chain fatty acids, which fight systemic inflammation and bad bacteria in the gut. By just adding 5% resistant starch to your meal, you will increase your post meal fat burn with the majority of fat coming off your belly and hips.

Top Bean Choices
- Black Beans
- Kidney Beans
- Pinto Beans
- Navy Beans
- Lima Beans

Nuts and Seeds: Nuts and seeds meet all the healthy snacking requirements. They contain omega-3 fatty acids, amino acids like L-arginine (which is critical in the production of Human Growth Hormone, the fat-burning, lean muscle building hormone), antioxidants, fiber, magnesium and resistant starch. As an added bonus, they help protect you from heart disease, diabetes, and inflammation.

Top Nuts & Seeds Choices
- Walnuts
- Almonds
- Cashews
- Pecans
- Brazil nuts
- Macadamia nuts
- Flax seed
- Pumpkin Seed
- Sesame seed
- Sunflower seed

Green "Leafies": Leafy vegetables, more than other types of vegetables, play a significant role in decreasing your risk for diabetes, possibly due to the fiber and magnesium content. The high levels of iron in spinach and Swiss chard carry oxygen to your muscles. Leafy greens also block the formation of prostaglandins, which cause inflammation, arthritic pain and blood clotting.

Top Green "Leafies" Choices
- Swiss Chard
- Turnips
- Organic Kale
- Organic Spinach
- Asparagus

Cruciferous Vegetables: These veggies pack serious nutritional power in every mouthful. They also have fewer calories due to their high water and fiber content. I think we've established that FIBER IS GOOD. Fiber fills you up and can increase your body's ability to burn fat.

Top Cruciferous Choices
- Organic Kale
- Collard greens
- Broccoli
- Cabbage
- Brussels sprouts
- Cauliflower

Colorful fruits and vegetables: Don't just eat green veggies, you need colorful fruits and vegetables, too. They contain essential vitamins, minerals, fiber, folate, potassium, lycopene, and vitamins A and C. These vitamins, minerals, and fiber help steady blood sugar levels, balance hormones and offer protection from chronic diseases.

Top Colorful Fruits and Veggies Choices
- Tomato
- Carrots
- Sweet Potato
- Avocado
- Purple plums
- Red grapefruit
- Red Onions
- Organic apples

Berries: Tangy, succulent berries arrive in the spring and summer, dangling from vines and bushes, waiting to be plucked and savored. While they're in season and tasting their best, take advantage and devour them by the bowlful. Rich in disease-fighting nutrients, berries rank among the healthiest fruits. Like wine and chocolate, berries have antioxidant qualities; but without the alcohol and caffeine. Berries have nutrients and fiber that keep your blood sugar from spiking. They make a sweet treat that can actually help you with your weight management goals.

Top Berry Choices
- Organic Blueberries
- Organic Strawberries
- Bilberries
- Blackberries
- Cranberries
- Raspberries

Unprocessed Whole Grains: Most people don't realize the power of whole grains. Part of their power comes from their fiber, resistant starch (RS1) and oligosaccharides. Resistant starch and oligosaccharides pass through the small intestine and are fermented in the colon. They function as "prebiotics" the food on which healthy bacteria [probiotics] thrive. Healthy bacteria produce short-chain fatty acids such as butyric acid. Butyric acid fights colon cancer cells while it simultaneously feeds healthy cells in the colon. Healthy colon cells help the body detox from pharmaceuticals and other environmental chemicals. The short-chain fatty acids from whole grains stimulate fat cells in our stomachs to release leptin, the satiety hormone. This means you will eat less.

Top Grain Choices
- Quinoa
- Buckwheat
- Millet
- Steel cut oats
- Barley

Meat and Dairy: When it comes to building lean muscle in your body, animal protein rules. Those of you who are 'veggie only' people might be cringing right now, but here are the facts. Animal protein has all 9 essential amino acids. Essential amino acids must be eaten, as the body does not produce them. Plant-based proteins DO NOT contain all 9 essential amino acids. Those 9 essential amino acids [Histidine, Isoleucine, Lysine, Methionine, Phenylalanine, Threonine, Tryptophan, Valine, and Leucine] are needed for muscle growth and maintenance, blood sugar regulation, alertness, appetite suppression, sleep, relaxation, and circulation. Meat products contain some other important non-essential amino acids, as well, such as: L-arginine, which is critical in the production of Human Growth Hormone (the fat burning, lean muscle building hormone), and Tyrosine, which helps control your appetite and reduces body fat.

Top Meats & Poultry Choices
- Organic lean cuts of beef include the tenderloin, round or center cut
- Organic Poultry – chicken

Top Dairy Choices
- Organic eggs. Eggs provide vitamins, minerals and amino acids in perfect balance.
- Organic Plain "Greek" Yogurt. Some brands give you twice the amount of protein than regular yogurt and have added probiotics that help maintain balance in your digestive tract and boost your immune system.

Fish: There are two major challenges with fish.

- **Toxicity**: Fish fat lodges the deadly toxins absorbed from the water where the fish is taken. Industrial waste is floating around the shores of America, and pesticides are sprayed into the ponds where farm-raised fish is kept.

- **Omega 3 levels**: Much of the salmon found on grocery shelves is farm-raised. Unless indicated, farm-raised fish has not been fed a natural ocean-based diet. They have been fed corn and grains. This increases the pro-inflammatory omega 6 fatty acids, and decreases the usable healthy omega 3.

All things considered, sometimes the safest route to ensure you get adequate omega 3's is to take a supplement and choose your fish carefully.

Top Fish Choices
- Mackerel
- Sardines
- Salmon
- Hoki fish
- Trout
- Tuna

Oils and butters: The rule of thumb is to avoid overcooking your food. Steam or lightly fry, as much as possible.

Top Oils and Butters
- Olive Oil
- Nut butters [these can help give you a sense of fullness so you don't overeat].

Top Seasonings
- Sea salt
- Black pepper
- Vinegar
- Garlic
- Cinnamon
- Basil
- Chili peppers
- Cumin seeds
- Ginger
- Oregano
- Sage
- Turmeric [curcumin]

Top Supplement Choices
- Multivitamin/minerals - preferably isotonic
- High-Quality Omega 3 from fish oil. Look for micro-distilled fish oil derived from small fish such as anchovies and sardines. It should be fished from bio-sustainable, pure waters [such as off the coast of Peru]. The amount of omega 3 should be designated on the label per capsule.

- As needed to support specific health goals:
    - Antioxidants
    - B complex
    - Adrenal support
    - Sleep support
    - Weight management support
    - Bone health
    - Blood sugar management

For menu ideas and a printable grocery list visit: www.lydiamartinez.com.

BUTT STEP THREE:

FOLLOW THE RULES

Abiding by these rules will help you achieve and maintain
a healthy weight. Even more importantly, you will have the
energy and mental focus you need to succeed - one meal at
a time, one snack at a time.

If you are struggling with an eating disorder or another medical issue, adhere to the recommendations of your supervising health professional.

Whether you are overweight, underweight, or spot on, these important rules apply. Abiding by these rules will help you achieve and maintain a healthy weight. Even more importantly, you will have the energy and mental focus you need to succeed - one meal at a time, one snack at a time.

Rule #1: Eat!

Are you one of those people who starve yourself all day and then inhale one large meal in the evening? You can NO LONGER do that! To stoke your muscle-building, energy-creating, fat-burning fires you need to eat the GOOD STUFF every 3-4 hours.

Eating creates something called the 'thermic effect'. This refers to the energy expended when you eat. Breaking your food down into nutrients accounts for 10% of the energy you expend during the day. In other words, the mere act of eating helps stoke your fat-burning fires [a.k.a. the metabolic process]. If you skip meals, you lose that edge.

You will be amazed at how changing this one behavior can give you full tilt energy and mental clarity almost immediately.

Rule #2: Eat until you're full.

You need to eat slowly until you feel full. I don't mean STUFFED! Don't eat until you are bloated and need to loosen your belt. Eat until you have that 'satisfied' feeling. Some of you, due to years of chronic overeating, have lost touch with what 'satisfied' feels like. [We will address that later.]

And I'm not talking about eating crap. By now, you know about the cycle of cravings that crap-food sets in motion. I'm talking about the good stuff: healthy, fresh, whole foods - not too little and not too much. When you're eating the right foods (lean protein, veggies, and good fats), it's kind of hard to overeat.

Rule #3: Eat breakfast within an hour of waking up - NO EXCUSE!!

Eating breakfast jump starts your metabolism and prevents an energy lag later in the day. As you sleep, about 80% of your energy stores [glycogen] are used up. It doesn't take long to go through that last 20%. If you are not eating breakfast, your body begins to use lean muscle for energy.

A healthy breakfast also helps to prevent binge eating. Binging is the result of blood sugar falling and stress hormones elevating. This triggers cravings for sugar, salt and fat. This vicious cycle contributes to Type 2 diabetes, and the diseases that accompany it.

So consider a healthy breakfast to be the first line of defense in protecting your body from degenerative disease and lean muscle loss.

Rule #4: Drink at least 2 quarts of water each day.

It is important for you to drink water each day – REAL water. Not water that has flavor and sugar added. Water helps keep you energized and clean on the inside. It also keeps your skin cells plump and youthful. Water will also support your fat-burning capabilities. It's the liver's job to convert stored fat into energy. Unfortunately, it is also the liver's job to pick up the slack for the kidneys when they are not detoxing the body

Abide By The Rules

efficiently. The kidneys need plenty of water to work properly. If the kidneys are water-deprived, the liver has to do their work along with its own. This means, its fat-burning energy is siphoned off into other tasks. A good rule of thumb is to drink no less than 2 quarts [8 eight ounce glasses] of filtered water each day. [The water in your coffee does not count]!

Rule # 5: Plan your meals and snacks.

For meal planning visit: www.lydiamartinez.com.

It will take about 30 minutes to plan your meals for the week. It is well worth the time commitment. When you plan what you're going to eat for each meal and snack you are less likely to binge on "junk" food.

Eating 'out' should not be the centerpiece of your meal plan. Restaurant food at its healthiest often contains excess sodium and hidden fat. It is more expensive, too. Why not eat at home [or pack your lunch] and invest the money you save into the training, the clothes and the tools you need to succeed?

COACH LYDIAS' EYEBALL METHOD
You don't need a calculator to know how much to eat. Commonsense and a look at your plate will tell you what you need to know. There should be protein and fiber at each meal. If you are exercising a lot or if you are a man, you might need a bit more food on your plate to feel satisfied.

Here is a rough idea of what you are aiming for.

THE MAIN MEALS [on your plate]

A palm size serving of protein [fish, chicken, lean beef, eggs]
A tight fist full of whole grains or starchy whole foods [i.e. potatoes]
The rest of the plate is filled with veggies

SNACKS

A handful of good food [fruit, veggies, nuts and seeds, a slice of turkey, yogurt]
Again, remember protein and fiber [from veggies and fruit] with each snack.

SAMPLE MENU

Breakfast: 7:30am- 9:30am (eat within the first hour of waking up]
1 cup Steel Cut Oats (w/skim organic milk)
½ cup berries
1 whole egg or 2 egg whites (cooked)

Snack: 11:00am-11:30am
Apple and a few almonds, a turkey slice or a protein bar

Lunch: 12:30pm-1:30pm
A palm-sized piece of grilled chicken or fish,
A plate full of grilled veggies (broccoli, asparagus, or your choice)
or salad greens w/added tomatoes, cucumbers, carrots, etc.

Snack: 4:30pm- 5:30 pm
½ cup of cottage cheese, plain Greek yogurt, or
almond slivers

Dinner: 7:30pm- 8:30pm
A palm-sized piece of grilled chicken,
A plate full of veggies (again your choice)
 including a sweet potato (with cinnamon or nutmeg - NO brown sugar!)

Note: In time-tight situations (when you can't stick to your plan) DO NOT GO HUNGRY. EAT!
Choose the healthiest option from the choices you have.

Tip: Keep a canister of mixed nuts (almonds, cashews, pistachios) in your car or office. Apples,
oranges and bananas can also be lifesavers. When you are on a tight schedule, but need to eat,
you can grab one of these.

Be warned, having these 'emergency snacks' available can tempt you to mindlessly munch. Make sure your body [not your emotions] is telling you to eat. To help prevent over-eating, store these foods conveniently, but not temptingly close.

> *Be warned, having these 'emergency snacks' available can tempt you to mindlessly munch. Make sure your body [not your emotions] is telling you to eat.*

Rule # 6: Don't eat carbs after 9 PM.

If you must eat late, due to your schedule, stay away from starchy carbs [potatoes, breads] and grains. Your ability to process sugar (glucose) gets weaker as the day goes by. About an hour after you fall asleep, your body releases its largest pulse of HGH (Human Growth Hormone). HGH is a fat-burning, muscle building hormone. Insulin inhibits HGH production. If you eat carbs, this will drive up your insulin levels and interfere with the work of this important hormone.

Rule #7: Know thyself.

These basic rules apply to most of us, but there are special circumstances that require tweaking. It is not the mission of this book to address special cases. That needs to be addressed by a qualified health professional, but here are some conditions that might require an adjustment to your meal plan.

Food Sensitivities

If you find yourself feeling tired, bloated and achy after a meal, you might have a food sensitivity or an allergy that needs to be addressed. Be sure to go to a knowledgeable health professional for allergy testing.

Carb Sensitivity

When eaten, carbohydrates are converted to glucose (blood sugar). Bottom-line, carbs equal sugar. As you know, with carbs 'slower is better'. The slow break down of carbs into sugar, to fuel your immediate energy needs is good. However, for some of you, even good carbohydrates will spike your insulin levels, and set in motion fat storage. This is called carbohydrate sensitivity. I know-- it's not fair!

If you think only the overweight are carb sensitive - you are wrong. I tend to prefer carbohydrates over protein. (Hey! What do you expect? I'm half Mexican. I grew up with tortillas and rice at every meal). I didn't think carbs were a problem for me. After all, I was in decent shape and very active. But I did notice, when I ate grains or starchy carbs, I felt bloated. Worse yet, despite my active schedule, I began gaining weight. I discovered, I am carb sensitive and I needed to adjust my meals and snacks accordingly.

To discover if you are carb sensitive - tune in:

- Do you feel bloated gassy and puffy after eating a carbohydrate [even a seemingly healthy whole grain bread, sweet potato or fruit]?
- Do you feel fatigued and foggy brained frequently?
- Do you have trouble losing weight, though you are eating well?

If so, you might be carb sensitive. The keys to overcoming carb sensitivity include:

- Exercise [The more muscle you have, the better you can process carbs]
- Weight reduction [if you are overweight]
- Limiting grains
- Limiting starchy carbs [potatoes, pastas]
- Limiting your fruit intake
- Limiting saturated fats [Fats make the cells less permeable to receiving nutrients from your food, including blood sugar]
- Supplementation: Make sure you are getting adequate B vitamins, chromium, selenium and vanadium. These are all important cofactors in metabolizing carbohydrates. You might also want to research herbal supplements that have been shown to enhance carb metabolism.

Gluten Sensitivity

Gluten comes from the same Latin root as "glue". This 'glue' gives elasticity to dough and provides the chewy, fluffy texture of bread products.

Gluten is a protein contained in wheat, rye, and barley. It is also part of the genetic structure of spelt, durum, semolina, kamut, couscous, and triticale. Gluten can show up in seemingly unlikely food items such as bouillons and soy sauces. It is important to check labels carefully to make sure there are no gluten products listed there. [If it says 'wheat', it has gluten].

Gluten sensitivity makes life uncomfortable. It causes bloating & diarrhea. The ongoing irritation of gluten will eventually damage the nutrient-absorbing villi in the small intestines and create lesions and chronic inflammation in the lining of the colon. [Another term used for one who has gluten sensitivity and a damaged intestinal tract is 'Celiac']. This damage leads to mal-absorption of nutrients and impaired elimination.

Some symptoms of gluten sensitivity include:

- Constant hunger
- Impaired weight management [cannot lose or cannot gain weight]
- Bloated belly

- IBS [Irritable Bowel Syndrome]
- Chronic skin problems

The good news is, eating a gluten-free diet will clear up these symptoms. If you have a gluten-sensitivity, you will notice a big difference when you stop eating gluten. Likewise, if you eat a gluten-containing food, the symptoms will return with a vengeance.

BUTT STEP FOUR:

MOVE YOUR MASS

You can enjoy many of the benefits of exercise just by intentionally moving more – taking a daily walk with a friend, dancing harder, playing with the kids more often, and loving your partner more passionately. All of these things are a powerful step in the right direction. Start there.

If you are just starting an exercise program or are coming back after some time off, or if you are being treated for a medical condition, be sure to check with your health professional before beginning an exercise program.

You chose this book because you want to reach beyond mediocrity in your life. You have goals. If you are going to create the focused, consistent energy you need to reach those goals, exercise MUST be a priority. No bones about it — You must MOVE YOUR MASS!!!!

Before we get started, let's dispel some myths that could be standing in the way of your commitment to exercise.

MYTH: You must work out hard and often, otherwise it is not worth exercising at all.

This kind of thinking keeps a lot of people from maintaining or even starting an exercise program. Research shows that any exercise is better than none. For example, regular walking or gardening, for as little as an hour a week, has been shown to reduce the risk of heart disease.

MYTH: Exercise Is one sure way to lose all the weight you desire.

Not true. Weight gain or loss is impacted by many factors, including the types of food you eat, how much food you eat and how often you eat it.

MYTH: Home workouts are fine, but going to the gym is best.

Research has shown that some people find it easier to stick to a home-based fitness program. Don't be swayed by the hype about trendy exercise programs and facilities. The "best" program for YOU is the one YOU will participate in consistently.

MYTH: Strength-training will make women too muscular.

Don't worry about looking like a bodybuilder. Women don't have enough testosterone to create big, bulky muscles. To become a bodybuilder, women have to do a lot of weird things that most strength-training programs don't do.

The fact is, strength-training is not only for men. Women need it too! Women naturally have less bone and muscle than men. That's why women are at greater risk of osteoporosis than men. Muscle-loss puts women at greater risk of disability as they age. Strength training increases lean muscle mass.

<u>MYTH: Thin people do not need to exercise.</u>

There are a lot of 'skinny-fat' people in the world. They appear thin, but the relative proportion of fat to muscle is high [aka body fat percentage]. The butt sags, the shoulders stoop, the arms flap and the belly bulges because they have little lean muscle. 'Skinny-fat' people need to incorporate exercise into their day just as much as a person who is overweight.

<u>MYTH: If you didn't exercise when you were younger, it's too late.</u>

It is never too late to start an exercise routine. You can reap benefits at any age. Exercise actually slows down the aging process. It reduces the loss of bone and muscle and increases the ability to move with youthful grace.

Exercise

<u>MYTH: Age and hormones make us fat.</u>

So many people blame their bulging belly and sluggish metabolism on age and hormones. That's malarkey! True, as we age our hormones shift in ways that encourage weight gain.

- The leptin receptors in the brain start to decrease, so your body doesn't recognize when it's full. This can lead to overeating.
- In women, female hormones decrease and insulin regulating hormones are less effective. This can lead to more fat (muffin top).
- In men, testosterone levels decline. Muscle mass and energy level can decrease. Belly fat and insulin resistance can increase.

These hormonal shifts not only contribute to a changing body shape, but they can also make you more irritable and depressed. Age doesn't excuse crankiness, nor does it excuse getting fat. The truth is, eating properly and exercising regularly can prevent and reverse obesity no matter your age.

Now that you have addressed the myths – let's talk about the facts.

<u>FACT: Your doctor probably recommends it.</u>

I have never had a client come back to me to tell me the doctor said," There's no science behind exercise and you don't need it."

FACT: Exercise helps balance moods.

It regulates the 'stress' hormone [cortisol] and stimulates the 'feel good' hormones [serotonin and dopamine].

FACT: Exercise burns fat.

It increases the fat burning hormones [i.e. Testosterone, HGH (human growth hormone), DHEA, and thyroxin (T4)].

FACT: Exercise improves cognitive function.

To get on with your life, you need a sharp mind, too. Exercise increases the blood flow and oxygen levels in the brain. These spikes are associated with a sharpened memory, heightened focus, creativity and problem solving. (And you thought 'Gym rats' were muscle-headed Neanderthals?)

FACT: Exercise prevents and even reverses degenerative disease.

Do your own research. You will find adequate exercise is associated with stronger bones, stabilized blood sugar, healthy arteries, lean bodies, less fat and all the other conditions needed to prevent, manage [or reverse] heart disease, diabetes, and cancer.

FACT: And there is more.

It reduces risk of addiction relapse. It promotes a healthier digestion. It reduces stiffness, aches and pains. It increases resistance to viral and bacterial infections and slows the aging process [Yes! Fewer wrinkles.]

FACT: You don't have to spend 6 hours a day in the gym.

Many popular fitness reality shows suggest that the only way to get fit is to organize your life around your exercise schedule. Like who has the luxury of doing that, right?

As a matter of fact, just like dieting, if exercise is temporarily "extreme", so are its benefits. In as little as 30 minutes of exercise, 5 days a week, you can see dramatic changes. Likewise, every day that you don't get up and move 'with purpose', you are one step closer to heart disease, diabetes, hypertension, cancer, depression, arthritis and osteoporosis.

So, there you have it. Exercise can improve your appearance, stabilize your moods, sustain your ambition and help you live longer. What is not to like?

Are you ready to roll? I hope so, because, you are in driver's seat. You decide how far and how fast you want to go with your fitness program.

START NOW

You can enjoy many of the benefits of exercise just by intentionally moving more – taking a daily walk with a friend, dancing harder, playing with the kids more often, and loving your partner more passionately. All of these things are a powerful step in the right direction. Start there.

The goal of any training session is simple.

• Incinerate Fat
• Tone and Build Muscle

TAKE IT UP A NOTCH

Diversify your exercise options. Get on a treadmill, elliptical or stationary bike. Visit the local pool, tennis court or local park. You might want to attend yoga or a martial arts class. These are a great ways have fun while you reduce stress and increase your strength and flexibility.

GO FOR THE GOLD

However, if you want a noticeably stronger, toner body with curves in all the 'right' places, you need to get off your dopah (a.k.a. butt) and really work it! Trust me, I know what it takes. My journey required commitment, sweat and discipline.

YOUR GOAL

The goal of any training session is simple.

- Incinerate Fat
- Tone and Build Muscle

To do this you need to maximize your fat-burning throughout the day, even when you are NOT exercising. It's called 'After burn'. The technical term is EPOC (Excess Post Oxygen Consumption).

'After burn' [EPOC] means that even 'after 'your exercise is done, your body continues to 'burn' fat. It works like this. When you challenge the oxygen levels in your body [It looks a lot like huffing and puffing], your body will break down your fat to use for fuel. The more intense and consistent your exercise is, the faster you burn fat and oxygenate your body. Exercise is like using bellows to stoke the flames in your fireplace. Once stoked, they keep burning.

During 'After burn' [EPOC] your body is:

- Replenishing energy stores (such as Adenosine Triphosphate and muscle glycogen)
- Re-oxygenating the blood
- Restoring the body temperature levels to a pre-exercise state
- Restoring pre-exercise breathing and heart-rate levels

In other words, restoring the body to its pre-exercise state is 'work'. And work means additional-al expenditure of energy [calories] beyond the energy consumed to perform that work.

'AFTER BURN' [EPOC] FACTS

1. All types of exercise (cardiovascular, strength, circuit and interval) will produce "after burn", although at different levels.

2. You can burn the same number of calories during your workout as the next person, but if you work out with a higher intensity, your body will burn calories for a longer period of time than the person who worked out with less intensity.

3. Resistance [strength] training performed with intervals of high intensity has been shown to increase EPOC for up to twice as long. For experienced weight lifters, "after burn" can last up to 38 hours after exercise. They are fat-burning machines.

This is why shorter, high intensity sessions have become popular. They take less time, and sustain after burn [EPOC] longer. You get results, faster.

To summarize, if you want to burn more fat during and after sessions you need periods of increased intensity during your training session followed by lower intensity exercises. This is called Interval Training.

Interval training involves alternating high intensity exercise with low intensity recovery periods. Intensity can be increased in different ways:

- Add resistance [add weight or increase incline]
- Add speed [sprinting instead of walking]
- Add both speed and resistance

An example of Interval training:

1 minute of a high intensity exercise [sprinting] followed by 2 minutes of low intensity exercise [walking] and alternating between high intensity and low intensity several times for 15-30 min-utes. Take it up a notch by increasing the incline on which you are walking, periodically.
The idea is to work harder than usual in your high intensity intervals and to fully recover during the low intensity intervals.

HOW TO CONSTRUCT A FITNESS PLAN

COMMITMENT: 6 days a week for 30 minutes a day

Find **Coach Lydia's Interval Training Plan** and exercise demos at www.lydiamartinez.com. If you want to design a plan on your own, be sure to include these basic building blocks.

- **Dynamic Warm up**
  10 minutes before each session

- **Metabolic Session**
  Twice a week for 20-30 minutes

- **Functional Strength Session**
  Twice a week for 20-30 minutes

- **Active Rest**
  Once a week for 20-30 minutes

- **Stretch session**
  Once a week for 20-30 minutes

DYNAMIC WARM UP
[every training session for 10 minutes]

Your muscles need warming up to prevent injury and enhance your results. Don't skip this part, but also don't do maneuvers that cause pain.

BENEFITS: Prevents muscle injury and increases results.

DYNAMIC WARM UP EXERCISE OPTIONS:
- Squats
- Toy soldier march
- Shoulder rolls
- Alternating between front and back rolls
- Hamstring stretches
- High Knee Walks
- Butt Kick

PACE YOURSELF! Are you wiped out after the dynamic warm up? That's okay. If that's all you can do, stop there. Now, I don't mean wimp out. You do need to challenge yourself.

But if you are just getting started, this might be all you can handle. Combining this with intentionally moving more throughout the day is a great start. It's all about progression.

METABOLIC SESSION twice a week
[20-30 minutes]

These sessions involve quick bursts of high-intensity movement followed by brief periods of rest. For example sprint for 3 minutes, walk for 1, sprint for 3 minutes, walk for 1.

BENEFITS: Incinerates body fat.

METABOLIC EXERCISE OPTIONS:
- Jump Rope
- Spin
- Inclined Treadmill
- Treadmill Sprinting
- Hill Climbing

FUNCTIONAL STRENGTH SESSION twice a week
[20-30 minutes]

Functional strength exercises mimic the movements that you use in your daily life. This is done without weight-lifting machines.

- Machine-based exercises isolate muscles groups. This encourages unnatural movement for the human body with the purpose of exaggerating muscles for 'show.' This does not mean that there is no value in using machines. Just make sure the centerpiece of your session is functional exercise.

- Functional training can provide a 'show-worthy body' for sure, but one that can perform daily tasks with stamina and grace.

Functional strength training engages muscles you use to perform 'real life' tasks - lifting, pushing, pulling and walking. These tasks engage muscles on both sides of the body [sagittal plane] the front and the back [frontal plane] and the upper and lower torso [transverse plane].

If you have ever been to a physical therapist, you are familiar with this type of training. A physical therapists goal is to restore your ability to perform your daily tasks after surgery or injury. Thus, if a patient's job requires heavy lifting, rehabilitation would be targeted toward heavy lifting. If the patient were a parent of young children, it would be targeted toward moderate lifting and endurance. If the patient were a marathon runner, training would be targeted toward re-building endurance and flexibility.

BENEFITS: Builds beautiful muscles, strengthens bones and helps you move with grace.

FUNCTIONAL STRENGTH TRAINING EXERCISE OPTIONS:
[For exercise demos go to www.lydiamartinez.com]
- Push-ups
- Squats
- Planks - these are stationary exercises that force your body to stabilize itself in one position. This engages muscles running throughout the body – side to side, up and down, back and front.

ONE ACTIVE REST DAY
[20-30 minutes]

This is not a "couch potato" day. This is a day off to enjoy other forms of movement. You need to get your heart rate up during your 'active rest' sessions. This gets your blood flowing, bringing oxygen and nutrients to muscles that were broken down by working out. Don't overdo it and keep it fun!

BENEFITS: Prevents boredom and helps your body recover.

ACTIVE REST EXERCISE OPTIONS:
Team sports [basketball, volleyball, flag football]
Bike ride [not uphill]
Power walk
Swim [leisurely paced]
Yoga

ONE STRETCH DAY
(15-30 minutes)

Mindfully stretching throughout each day is important, but intentionally focus on stretching one day a week.

BENEFITS: Increases flexibility and range of motion, stress relief and enhanced coordination.

STRETCH OPTIONS:
Yoga
Pilates
Simply Stretching

DEVELOP A WEEKLY TRAINING ROUTINE

Here a sample of a 4 week training schedule. Note: You can either do the same type of exercise on a given day, or you can alternate to keep from getting bored and to keep the body 'on its toes.'

Monday	Tuesday	Wednesday	Thursday	Friday	Saturday	Sunday
Strength	Metabolic	Off	Strength	Metabolic	Active Rest	Stretch
Metabolic	Active Rest	Strength	Stretch	Metabolic	Off	Strength
Off	Strength	Metabolic	Active Rest	Strength	Stretch	Metabolic
Active Rest	Metabolic	Strength	Off	Stretch	Metabolic	Strength

DON'T STRIVE FOR PERFECTION, STRIVE FOR PROGRESSION

If you are just starting out, here is a way to work up.

Start with dynamic warm-up and then add 10 minutes on the treadmill.
- Progress: Work up to 20 to 30 minutes on the treadmill.
- Progress: Now add sprinting. Walk for 60 seconds – sprint for 10 seconds. When you can do this walk – sprint combination for at least 15 minutes, take it up a notch.
- Progress: Sprint longer relative to the walking. Walk for 60-seconds, sprint for 30 seconds. When you can do this for at least 15 minutes, take it up a notch.
- Progress: Now add strength training by increasing the incline you are walking on [treadmill or hill].

This is called 'Progressive Resistance' training. The key is to start and to progress.

EAT PROPERLY

Eating properly [the right foods, the right amounts, at the right time] is important for optimizing the effects of your training session, maximizing after-burn and refueling your body.

BEFORE WORKOUT

- Large meals: Wait 2-3 hours before exercising.
- Small meals: Wait 1-2 hours before exercising.
- Small snacks: Wait 15-30 minutes before exercising.

Eating too much before exercise can leave you feeling sluggish. Worse yet, you could end up with stomach cramps, vomiting and diarrhea. Eating too little short-changes the energy you need to feel strong throughout your workout.

AFTER WORKOUT

To help your muscles recover and to replace their glycogen stores, eat a meal that contains both protein and good carbs within 30 - 60 minutes of your exercise session. Options:

- Protein Shake
- Plain Greek yogurt and fruit (1 serving)
- Peanut butter and apple
- Nuts and dried fruit
- A regular meal with lean meat, grain (like ½ cup of quinoa), and cooked vegetable or salad

SAMPLE MENU FOR THOSE WHO WORK OUT IN THE MORNING

7:00 am - BREAKFAST
½ cup of cooked Steel Cut oatmeal, a few berries, 4-8 oz. egg whites, or 1 whole egg with chopped peppers and green onions. [Men may require more protein depending on their fitness goals].

My Fav: High Protein Buckwheat pancakes with a tablespoon of Greek yogurt and berries with an egg white omelet.

10:00 am - TRAIN

11:00 am - SNACK [post-training nutrition]
Protein Shake [optional: add banana or berries)

12:30 pm - LUNCH
Grilled Chicken or Fish with wild rice [or a ½ cup of quinoa] on a bed of romaine lettuce, with veggies, vinaigrette and an apple.

3:30 pm - SNACK
Protein Shake or Celery with peanut butter (sometimes I eat both, depending on the intensity of my training session)

6:00 pm - DINNER
4-8 oz. Chicken Breast or Fish with 1 cup of green beans, and 1 cup of other veggies (i.e. red peppers, asparagus, snap peas, or cauliflower)

8:00 pm - SNACK
A couple slices of turkey, 1/2 sweet potato (no brown sugar) or cottage cheese and veggies

SAMPLE MENU FOR THOSE WHO WORK OUT IN THE EVENING

7:00 am – BREAKFAST
½ cup of cooked Steel Cut oatmeal, a few berries, 4-8 oz. egg whites, or 1 whole egg with chopped peppers and green onions

11:00 am – SNACK
1 cup Greek plain yogurt with 2 large strawberries, 4 blackberries and almond slivers, ½ packet of Stevia to sweeten the yogurt [or apple/ celery with peanut butter]

12:30 pm – LUNCH
4-8 oz. Grilled Chicken or Fish with steamed veggies/green beans over quinoa, and side of cottage cheese sweetened with Stevia

4:00 pm – SNACK
Protein Shake or Turkey Wrap (whole grain) with grilled veggies

5:30 pm – TRAIN

6:30 pm – SNACK [post-training nutrition]
Protein Shake [optional: add banana or berries)

7:30 pm – DINNER
4-8 oz. Chicken Breast or Fish with 1 cup of green beans, and 1 cup of other veggies (i.e. red peppers, asparagus, snap peas, or cauliflower)

10:00 pm – SNACK
Protein Shake or a couple slices of turkey, 15 almonds and 1 slice of low fat cheese.

THINK LIKE AN ATHLETE

Here is some great advice from Coach Shannon Wallace, someone I consider to be among the top fitness trainers in the nation.

"Train like an athlete no matter who you are. Some people think that athletes are someone that jumps high, runs fast, and can catch a ball. That is a reality-disconnect. We all have the same biomechanics --we all sit, we all walk and we all stand. We can all train like an athlete.

The spirit of the athlete is this. They have a strong will to succeed, to win, and to finish the task. Can't is not part of the vocabulary. Athletes are goal-centered because they always begin with the end in mind.

If an athlete wants to win the Super Bowl, the World Series or a WNBA championship, they have a post season and pre-season conditioning. If they want to win an Olympic gold medal they train for four years.

The point is, if you want to be fit for your wedding or a vacation, for health reasons, or just to feel better about who you are - you can't do that in a day. It takes concerted effort, discipline and commitment to achieve what you want.

Just like an athlete, you must always be in the process of 'becoming'. You can't wait till the day comes to get ready - You must always be 'becoming'. The best part is – you are empowered - not just by your achievements - but by the journey along the way. Getting fit is a journey not just a destination. "

With Coach Shannon's words, ringing in your ears, let's get started.

BUTT STEP FIVE:

CULTIVATE A PEACEFUL MIND

We all experience stress.
Stress can be a positive force that motivates, or a negative
force that destroys.

DISCLAIMER: For those of you who are plagued with ongoing anxiety and dread that is inhibiting your ability to function, check with a knowledgeable health professional for treatment options.

We all experience stress. Stress can be a positive force that motivates, or a negative force that destroys.

The Biology of Stress

When you experience stress, the pituitary gland, a pea-sized gland nestled in your brain, releases a hormone called ACTH [adrenocorticotropin]. The ACTH travels through the bloodstream to the pair of adrenal glands located above the kidneys. The adrenal glands releases 3 stress hormones:

- Norepinephrine – The 'do it now' hormone
- Epinephrine – The 'anxiety' hormone
- Cortisol - The 'defeated' hormone

When we were hunters and gatherers, these potent chemicals increased our running speed to help us catch wild game or get out of the way of a stampeding buffalo herd. They kept us alive.

Though we no longer have to worry about fleeing buffalo stampedes, we still draw on these hormones to help us meet pressing deadlines or catch the glass that slips off the counter. Each of these stress hormones is released in different ratios based on the challenge we are facing.

- **Manageable, short term challenges**, such as running a race, or making a sales call, trigger the release of more norepinephrine relative to the other stress hormones. Norepinephrine is the 'do it now' hormone. It stops the production of insulin, the hormone that helps clean sugar out of your blood. This is so you have enough sugar for needed energy to fulfill the task.

- **Pressing but short-term challenges**, such as a traffic jam or company coming for dinner, trigger the release of more epinephrine relative to the other hormones. Epinephrine is the 'anxiety hormone'. It slows down your digestion and suppresses your appetite so that you can focus on the challenge at hand, rather than eating. This is one of the reasons stress goes hand in hand with gastrointestinal problems.

- **Chronic stress** triggers the release of more cortisol relative to the others. Cortisol is the 'hormone of defeat'. When you are continually overwhelmed, discouraged, and convinced there is no way out of your debt, your marriage issues, your illness, or your work overload; your body will be pulsing cortisol continually. Unlike the other stress hormones, cortisol's effects are long lasting. And those effects are very damaging.

Cortisol's Damage to Your Body

You Crave High Fat, High Carb, & Salty Foods

Cultivate a Peaceful Mind

While epinephrine's "adrenaline" rush can suppress your appetite, cortisol stimulates your appetite. If you never 'take a break from stress', cortisol levels remain elevated. This will trigger cravings for high fat, high carb and salty foods. Your leptin levels will decrease. Leptin is the hormone that tells the body it is full after eating. Essentially, cortisol creates an urge to overeat junk food. Once you eat, your body releases a cascade of rewarding brain chemicals – opioids. This creates a 'comfort food' addiction.

- You feel stressed.
- You crave junk.
- You overeat junk.
- You feel better.

If you don't consciously avoid this pattern, you can become physically and psychologically dependent on 'comfort' food to manage your stress.

You Store Fat

When stress continues for a long period of time and cortisol levels stay high, the body will resist weight loss. Your body is tricked into thinking 'times are hard' and there is a chance you might starve. To help you survive, it stores the sugar from your food in your fat cells. Cortisol will also turn adipocytes, immature fat cells, into mature fat cells that stay with you forever!!!!

Worse yet, cortisol can actually transport fat from healthier areas, like your butt and hips, and distribute it to your belly. It turns healthy peripheral fat – the fat that is used as cushioning - into unhealthy visceral fat – 'belly fat' that wraps around the body's organs. Visceral fat increases your risk for heart disease and type 2 diabetes. It impairs your brain function and it lowers your immunity. This makes you more vulnerable to everything from colds to cancer.

Belly fat is self-perpetuating. It becomes an easy storage site for fat. When cortisol signals the need to store fat, it sends it there. That's why it's so hard to get rid of those love handles!

Your Body Eats Your Lean Muscle

Once your stress has passed, cortisol tells the body to stop producing the stress hormones and to resume digestion. That is if you have normal levels of cortisol. But if you are under chronic stress, your cortisol levels remain elevated all the time. Excess cortisol has a big impact on your blood sugar, particularly on how your body uses sugar for energy.

Cortisol has another amazing power to tell your body which foods to burn for energy and which foods to store. If you need energy for short term stress, cortisol can take your fat, in the form of triglycerides, and move it to your muscles for more strength. If your stress is relentless, cortisol will break down your muscle tissue to release the stored sugar [glycogen] to use for energy.

Over time, it will not only break down your muscle but it will break down your skin [leading to easy bruising] and your bones [leading to osteoporosis].

Bottom line - Stress makes you sick, tired and fat. Say it with me ---UGH!

The Damage to your life

Equally tragic, stress causes a break down in our relationships with other people. Under stress you manifest unpleasant behaviors that distance you from others.

- You become irritable and intolerant of even minor disturbances.
- You lose your temper more often and yell at others for no reason.
- You feel jumpy or exhausted all the time.
- You find it hard to concentrate or focus on a task. This creates even more stress because you cannot seem to get things done.
- You worry too much about insignificant things.
- You doubt your ability to do things.
- You chew your nails or pull out your hair.
- You begin to imagine negative, worrisome, or terrifying scenes.
- You get depressed.

How to manage stress

Stress, however unpleasant, is a reality of life. It is part of being human.

Genetics do play a role in your response to stress. Yes, it's true; some of us are just mellower than others. Life experiences also affect the stress response. Those who have experienced trauma or chronic exposure to stress develop hyper-reactivity to stressful situations. For example, soldiers who have weathered wars or children who have been abused become hardwired to overreact to even minor threats that resemble past stressors.

Though you can't eliminate it from life, stress can be managed.

<u>Unhealthy ways to manage stress</u>

- Smoking
- Drinking too much
- Over eating or under eating
- Zoning out for hours in front of the TV/computer
- Withdrawing from friends, family and activities
- Using pills or drugs to relax
- Sleeping too much or procrastinating
- Filling up every minute of the day to avoid facing problems

<u>Healthy ways to manage stress</u>

1. <u>Acknowledge your role in perpetuating stress in your life.</u>

   - Do you explain away stress as temporary?

     "I just have a million things going on right now. When this passes I can relax."

   - Do you define stress as an integral part of your work or home life?

     "Things are always crazy around here!"

   - Do you identify with it as a part of your personality?

     "I have a lot of nervous energy, that's all."

   - Do you blame your stress on other people or outside events?

     "If it weren't for so and so, doing such and such, I wouldn't be stressed."

   - Do you view it as entirely normal and unexceptional?

     "Oh well. Such is life."

Accept responsibility for the role you play in creating or maintaining your stress. Until you do, your stress level will remain out of control.

2. <u>Tune into your stress cycles.</u>

   - Connect the dots between your tight shoulders, jumpiness and clenched jaw to stress. When you feel these things, acknowledge that you are in the grip of stress and it needs to be managed so that it does not damage your health.

- **Journal –** Writing things down can help you identify the patterns of stress in your life and the way you deal with them. Each time you feel stressed, ask yourself:

- What caused my stress? Venture a guess if you are unsure.
- How did I respond to that stress?
- Did my response make me feel better or worse?
- Was my response helpful or unproductive?
- Was my response healthy or unhealthy?
- What things can I do to break the stress cycles?

3. <u>Control what you can.</u>

- **Put together an action plan to deal with stressors** – If credit debt is keeping you awake at night - put together a debt reduction plan. If your weight is causing you anxiety and shame - put together a weight management plan.

- **Learn how to say "no"** – Know your limits and stick to them. Whether in your personal or professional life, refuse to accept added responsibilities when you're close to reaching your limit. Only you know your limit. Taking on more than you can handle is a surefire recipe for stress.

- **Avoid people who stress you out** – If someone consistently causes stress in your life and you can't turn the relationship around, limit the amount of time you spend with that person or end the relationship entirely.

- **Take control of your environment** – If the evening news makes you anxious, turn the TV off. If traffic's got you tense, take a longer but less-traveled route. If going to the market is an unpleasant chore, do your grocery shopping online.

- **Avoid hot-button topics** – If you get upset over religion or politics, cross them off your conversation list. If you repeatedly argue about the same subject with the same people, stop bringing it up or excuse yourself when it's the topic of discussion.

- **Pare down your to-do list** – Analyze your schedule, responsibilities, and daily tasks. If you've got too much on your plate, distinguish between the "should" and the "must." Drop tasks that aren't truly necessary to the bottom of the list or eliminate them entirely.

- **Manage your time better** – Poor time management can cause a lot of stress. When you're stretched too thin and running behind, it's hard to stay calm and focused. But if you plan ahead and make sure you don't overextend yourself, you can alter the amount of stress you're under.

- **Look at the big picture** – Get perspective on the stressful situation. Ask yourself how important it will be in the long run. Will it matter in a month? A year? Is it really worth getting upset over? If the answer is no, focus your time and energy elsewhere.

4. <u>Don't try to control the uncontrollable.</u>

Many things in life are beyond your control— particularly the behavior of other people. Rather than sitting around worrying and stressing out over things that are not under your control, focus on the things you can control such as the way you choose to react to problems. Once you identify a situation that is not under your control or that you can't change, 'let it go'. Find a way to occupy yourself with something else.

> *Many things in life are beyond your control— particularly the behavior of other people. Rather than sitting around worrying and stressing out over things that are not under your control, focus on the things you can control such as the way you choose to react to problems.*

5. <u>Take time to relax daily</u>.

Don't allow other obligations to encroach. This is your time to take a break from all responsibilities and recharge your batteries.

- **Spend time with your dog or cat**. Research shows that, when conducting a task that's stressful, people actually experienced less stress when their pets were with them! have no "official" study, but I had my Dalmatian, Buddie, for 17 years and I can truly say that he made my day, every day. The presence and energy a pet can bring to a home in the hardest of times is amazing. I believe animals have an innate ability to know exactly what you are going through.

- **Take advantage of the body's natural relaxation response**. It is a powerful antidote to stress. Relaxation techniques such as deep breathing, visualization, progressive muscle relaxation, meditation, and yoga can help you activate this relaxation response. When practiced regularly, these activities lead to a reduction in your everyday stress levels and a boost in your feelings of joy and serenity. What's more, they also serve a protective role by teaching you how to stay calm and collected in the face of life's future curveballs. In addition to its calming physical effects, research shows that the relaxation response also increases energy and focus, combats illness, relieves aches and pains, heightens problem-solving abilities, and boosts motivation and productivity.

- **Listen to music**. Did you know that listening to classical music while eating causes people to eat less, savor their food more, and digest more easily? So maybe it's time to learn to appreciate some good classical music.

- **Laugh and cry**. Expressing emotions can help you to blow off steam in a healthy way.

- **Spend time with positive people**. Go to a movie or dinner with a friend. Sometimes getting away and getting your mind off your problems can help you gain perspective.

- **Take a bath or shower**. Warm water soothes the body. As you lie in a warm tub or rinse off in a warm shower, imagine all the things stressing you out flowing into the water and down the drain.

- **Write, paint, or play music**. Creative activity is a good way to refocus and calm the mind.

6. Nourish your body.

Eating high-quality foods at regular intervals throughout the day will help your body to be able to sustain under pressure.

Make sure you are sensibly supplementing. Some supplements to consider with your health professional are:

- B complex: Supplementing with B-vitamins can support the important neuro-transmitters in the brain, such as serotonin, norepinephrine and dopamine. These hormones are important for supporting relaxation, motivation and stable moods.

- Omega 3 fatty acids [fish oil]: These essential fats are important to the formation of healthy neuro-receptors in the brain. You need well formed receptors to receive those important neuro-transmitters mentioned above.

As you manage stress, your energy levels will rise, your relationships with others will improve and your ability to stay focused on your life purpose will be sharpened.

BUTT STEP SIX:

SLEEP TIGHT

Sleep is more than simply a period of rest; it is an essential time for your body to perform routine maintenance, create long-term memories and repair damage from your day.

If insomnia is ongoing and negatively impacting the quality of your life, seek the counsel of a health professional. A cumulative sleep deficit can result in serious health consequences over time.

We all know that a healthy diet and exercise are keys to good health, but remember that the right quantity of high-quality sleep is just as crucial.

The Sleep Construction Crew

Sleep is more than simply a period of rest; it is an essential time for your body to perform routine maintenance, create long-term memories and repair damage from your day. Sleep brings many health benefits.

While you enjoy your rest, your body is hard at work. A construction crew consisting of various hormones are rebuilding and recalibrating your body.

Some things the crew does:
- Erase fine lines on your face
- Build bone
- Build lean muscle
- Heal tissue

In the morning you awake alert and energized, ready to roll.

On the other hand, if you are not giving them a full work day (7 + hours of sleep at night), inevitably there will be a deterioration of your health, both mental and physical. The consequences could include:

Immunity Compromised A 2009 study reported in the *Archives of Internal Medicine* suggests that those who sleep less than 7 hours per night were three times as likely to get sick as those who averaged at least 8 hours.

Weight Gain Lack of sufficient sleep tends to disrupt hormones that control hunger and appetite and the resulting daytime fatigue often discourages you from exercising.

Diabetes A 2009 report in *Diabetes Care* found people who had insomnia for a year or longer and who slept less than 5 hours per night had a threefold higher risk of type 2 diabetes. The underlying cause is thought to be the disruption of the body's normal hormonal regulation resulting from insufficient sleep.

Heart Disease A study published in the journal *Sleep*, notes that the risk of high blood pressure was three-and-a-half times greater among insomniacs who routinely slept less than 6 hours per night, compared with normal sleepers who slept 6 or more hours nightly.

Elevated Cancer Risk Research has shown a link between the increased risk for breast and colon cancer in shift workers that are working during normal sleeping hours. Light exposure reduces the level of melatonin, a hormone that both makes us sleepy and is thought to protect against cancer.

Sleep Tight

Memory Loss Researchers do not fully understand why we sleep and dream, but a process called memory consolidation occurs during sleep. While your body may be resting, your brain is busy processing your day by making connections between events, sensory input, feelings and memories. Your dreams and deep sleep are an important time for your brain to make memories and links.

Bottom line - Get 7 + hours of sleep every night. Experiment with the specific amount that feels good to you.

Then, be consistent.

Sleep Tips:

- **Exercise every day**. Even 20 minutes of walking can help keep stress hormones from interfering with your sleep.

- **Avoid large meals just before bedtime**. An active digestive system can disrupt sleep.

- **Avoid caffeine, nicotine or other stimulants** within 4 hours of bedtime.

- **Avoid before-bed snacks, particularly grains and sugars**. This will raise blood sugar and inhibit sleep. Later, when blood sugar drops too low (hypoglycemia), you might wake up and not be able to fall back asleep.

- **Minimize noise and temperature extremes**. Your bedroom should be comfortably cool, about 68 degrees.

- **Don't read, watch television or work in bed**. Use the bed only to sleep. This helps prevent you from developing sleep disorders.

- **Listen to white noise or relaxation CDs**. Some people find the sound of white noise or nature sounds, such as the ocean or forest, to be soothing for sleep.

- **Sleep in complete darkness or as close as possible**. The presence of light lowers your pineal gland's production of melatonin, the sleep hormone. Make sure there is as little light in the bathroom as possible if you get up in the middle of the night. As soon as you turn on a bright light you cease production of melatonin.

- **Wear socks to bed**. Due to the fact that they have the poorest circulation, the feet often feel cold before the rest of the body. A study has shown that wearing socks to bed reduces night waking.

- **Consider supplementation**. The following supplements have been shown to be helpful to some. Consider your options with a knowledgeable health professional.

  B Complex B vitamins are important for stress management, and we know stress can interfere with sleep.

  Calcium has a sedative effect on the body. A calcium deficiency in the body causes restlessness.

  Magnesium deficiency can contribute to restlessness that prevents sleep.

  Chromium is often effective for someone with a blood sugar problem that is keeping them awake at nights.

  Tryptophan (L-tryptophan) In the brain, tryptophan is converted into serotonin, a natural sleep-inducing chemical. It also enhances the brain's ability to produce melatonin, the hormone that regulates your body's natural inner clock. L-tryptophan is found in foods such as milk and turkey.

  Melatonin The "darkness hormone," is secreted naturally by the pineal gland in the absence of light. Melatonin is found naturally in plants and in algae. In several studies, supplementation with melatonin has been found helpful in inducing and maintaining sleep. However, it appears melatonin supplementation will only produce a sedative effect when the person taking it has low melatonin levels. If melatonin levels are not deficient, there is little to no effect.

Passion flower *has a long history of use for symptoms of restlessness, mood disorders or emotional problems.*

Chamomile *has been used for centuries to treat insomnia and for its calming and sedative effects.*

BUTT STEP SEVEN:

STAY ON TRACK

The journey toward good health is straightforward:

- Don't do the things that lead to poor health.
    - Do the things that lead to good health.

The problem is:

- The 'wrong things' are so easily accessible.
    - The 'right things' take effort.

Warning: If you are locked into patterns of extreme behavior regarding eating and fitness, starving yourself, binging and purging or excessive overeating, it is important for you to get the help you need. Check the recommended resources section for suggestions.

The journey toward good health is straightforward:

- Don't do the things that lead to poor health.
- Do the things that lead to good health.

The problem is:

- The 'wrong things' are so easily accessible.
- The 'right things' take effort.

Then there is the 'denial' component. Connecting the dots between what you are doing today and its effect on your health tomorrow is difficult. Diet and lifestyle-related disease is hidden and progressive. Eating a donut is not like eating poison. You don't suddenly collapse on the floor with the first bite. It takes years of eating the wrong things before you enter a disease state.

Despite these challenges, you need to seriously consider the consequences of your choices. Inattention to these critical matters destroys you. Not just your physical life, it affects your bottom line, too. If you, like millions of Americans, are under-insured, one serious incident could wipe you out financially.

There is another, more patriotic reason, to 'clean up your act'. Universal health care is on the national agenda. Many of the diseases clogging our health care system are related to personal choice. Yes, it is a good thing for all Americans to have access to the health care they need, but our nation can't afford a bailout program for personal irresponsibility.

So, there are 3 good reasons to change your diet and lifestyle habits. If you don't make some changes you could face the following consequences:

- Physical impairment
- Premature death
- Financial ruin for you [and your nation!]

Enough tough talk. The good news is - there is abundant grace in the journey. Your body is amazingly resilient;The ability to restore itself, profound. Most of us can weather dozens of donut over a lifetime with little damage. It is only when you allow your occasional lapses to grow into a lifestyle that you begin to wreak serious damage on your body.

So, how do get in the habit of making healthy decisions – most of the time!!!

Let's get started. Grab a glass of water, or a cup of tea. Get some writing utensils or a laptop. You are going to drill deep down into your motivation for getting fit and healthy. If you are serious about getting healthy, do not skip this step.

WHERE AM I NOW?

Stay On Track

- **THE MIRROR TEST**: This is best done with little or no clothes on. You are not allowed to hold in your gut and turn at a flattering angle. First accept that God gave you a basic body type. Each type is beautiful in its unique way. You are not going to change your basic proportions, but you do need to strive to be in the best shape that you can be. So, ask yourself:

What evidence that I am out of shape shows up when I look in the mirror? Examples: Bulging mid-riff. Soft arms. Double chin. Stooping shoulders. Ribs showing. Butt muscles sagging.

- **THE FITNESS/MEDICAL TEST**: Diet and lifestyle related disease kills. For example, it is estimated 1 American dies of heart disease every minute of the day. Degenerative diseases, like type 2 diabetes and heart disease, creep up on you and then eat you alive. You need to take any sign of an impending problem seriously.

What medical problems or physical limitations are beginning to surface due to my diet and lifestyle? Examples: Can't walk up stairs. High blood pressure. Poor sleep. Lack of energy.

- **THE EMOTIONAL PAIN TEST**: Poor health and an unfit body affect your self-image. Your self-image is reflected in your emotions and behaviors. Shame, depression, dread and insecurity deflate the joy of living.

What emotions am I experiencing due to my physical condition? Examples: Embarrassment makes me hate to be naked in front of my partner. I wear concealing clothes even on a hot day. I dread going to PTA meetings with my kid.

WHERE DO I WANT TO BE?

To get what you want, you have to decide what you want. A goal statement is a written vision of what you want. To help you crystallize what you want, ask yourself:

- *What does a fit body, for me, look like? Examples: Toned arms. Defined waist. Defined jaw line. Nice curves. Not too bony.*

- *What does good health, for me, mean? Examples: Cholesterol down. Reduced medication.*

- *What does a good self-image feel like? Examples: I have more enthusiasm for the future. I am more outgoing.*

WHAT DO I WANT AND WHEN?

With that vision in mind, write a goal statement. Write it out in 1 month, 3 month, 6 month and 1 year increments. For example:

CURRENT CONDITION: I can barely squeeze into a size 14 now.
- *At the end of 30 days, my size 14 fits scomfortably.*
- *At the end of 90 days, I am a size 12.*
- *At the end of 6 months, I am a size 10.*
- *At the end of the year, I am a size 8.*

CURRENT CONDITION: I cannot walk up the stairs at work without stopping twice to take a breath.
- *At the end of 30 days, I am able to walk up those stairs without stopping.*
- *At the end of 90 days, I am able to walk up those stairs 3 times in a row without stopping.*
- *At the end of 6 months, I am able to walk 1 mile comfortably.*
- *At the end of 1 year, I am able to walk 3 miles comfortably.*

PUT YOUR GOAL THROUGH A REALITY CHECK
Ask yourself these questions for each change you want to make.

- *Do I believe reaching this goal is possible?*
- *Do I have a passionate desire to make this change?*
- *Am I willing to commit the time/resources necessary to achieve this goal?*
- *Am I ready to get started now?*

If you can answer 'Yes!' to those 4 questions, the likelihood of staying committed to your goal is high. If you cannot, it would be better for you to identify a goal that aligns with your timing, belief and desire. Achieve that goal first. This will give you the confidence necessary to take on bigger challenges.

DEFINE YOUR REASON WHY We, humans, are drawn toward pleasure and repelled by pain. If the pleasure of NOT changing is greater than the pleasure of changing you will settle for the way things are. Likewise, if the pain of NOT changing is greater than the pain of changing, you will be motivated to change. Identify those motivators.

> *Living a healthy lifestyle is simple, but not easy. Most of the health challenges we have could be prevented or reversed by a few, very simple, changes.*

PLEASURE TEST: What will it feel like when I reach my goal?

Example: I no longer have to design my vacation around my inability to walk up stairs. My productivity has increased now that I no longer require a nap in the middle of the day. I now have enough energy to volunteer at the woman's shelter once a week. My partner is proud of me. I can see it in his eyes. I wear trendy clothes and enter a room confidently.

PAIN TEST: What will it feel like if I don't ?

Example: I sit on the sidelines of life due to lack of energy, weight issues and pain. My healthy friends enjoy active vacations, while I stay at home. It is likely that I will not see my grandchildren graduate from college due to my type 2 diabetes and heart disease. I am not advancing in my profession because of my moodiness and inability to stay focused.

With that vision in mind, write out your reason WHY.
Don't worry about eloquence, just write it down.

Example: My mom died of degenerative heart disease in her 50's with all the same health problems I have. I am now 48. If I die in my 50's I will not see my grandchildren graduate from college, get married and have children of their own. I want to enjoy an active and purpose driven retirement, not dread each day due to disability and pain.

DEVELOP YOUR ACTION PLAN
Living a healthy lifestyle is simple, but not easy. Most of the health challenges we have could be prevented or reversed by a few, very simple, changes.

- Eat good food rather than junk food.
- Eat every 3-4 hours rather than starving and then binging.
- Exercise 30 minutes a day rather than zoning out in front of a screen.
- Drink 2 quarts of water through the day, rather then sweet drinks.
- Manage stress rather than self-medicating with food or alcohol.
- Go to bed at a decent time rather than burning the midnight oil.

There is personalization within these changes. For example, you can choose from a variety of foods. You can choose the level of exercise and types of exercise you are willing to commit to. You can manage your stress with a daily walk with your dog or a weekly yoga class. But those are the basics of what you need to stay fit and healthy.

PRE-EMPT OBSTACLES TO SUCCESS

The key is consistency. The more consistent you are in abiding by 'the rules', the faster and more solid your progress will be. Therein lies the problem. There is an initial rush of enthusiasm when you first make a decision to change; but then the challenges come, the doubts rush in and your commitment erodes. It's like you have two voices in your head.

One saying, *"You are going to nail it this time."* The other saying, *"I don't think so. You've tried this before. Do you remember last year? There you stood in front of the mirror, eyeing your thickening waist. You clenched your teeth and declared, 'This year, I am going to get in shape!' Oh yeah, and you rushed off to the store to buy spandex tights and a truck load of celery sticks. But lo and behold, you never made it past that New York cheese cake with the chocolate frosting? Remember?"*

Those voices haunt all of us, if we let them. That is why working through this process is so important. You increase your chances of success dramatically if:

- You have a realistic goal statement.
- You have a clearly defined reason why.
- You know what you need to do.
- AND you identify potential obstacles and develop a plan to overcome them.

List the behaviors or beliefs that were obstacles to your success in the past.

1. All or nothing mentality
2. Emotional eating
3. Financial constraints
4. Negative significant people like a spouse, parents, or friends
5. Traumatic, life changing event
6. Scheduling
7. Lack of planning
8. Lack of confidence in your ability to change
9. Weak, pity party excuses
10. And what about – that New York cheese cake?

Develop an action plan to overcome them.

Identifying your potential challenges and constructing a plan to pre-empt them gives you a sense of control. It postures you to overcome those challenges, rather than to be overcome by them.

Examples:

1. **All or nothing mentality**: I might not be ready to train for a marathon yet, but starting today I am going to increase the number of steps I take. I will take the stairs instead of the elevator. I will celebrate my choices to take more steps in my day.

2. **Emotional eating**: I am going to keep the junk food out of my environment.

3. **Financial constraints**: I am going to identify the money I waste on unhealthy activities and commit it to my lifestyle change.

4. **Negative significant people** [spouse, parents, friends, kids]: I am going to spend at least one evening a week with individuals who are on the same track that I am by joining a community walking club or starting my own 'get off your butt' accountability group.

5. **Traumatic, life changing event**: I cannot change the fact that my husband left me; but I can change my response to it. I am designing and embracing my new life of singlehood. My first step is to sign up for a Pilates class.

6. **Scheduling**: I will list on my calendar the things I need to do like pack my lunch and go to the park or the mall for a 30 minute walk during my lunch hour.

7. **Lack of planning**: I will plan my menu on Sunday evenings from 7-7:30 pm and shop on Monday after work. I will put my weekly grocery list into my purse so I don't leave home without it.

8. **Lack of confidence in my ability to change**: I will choose one thing to change that I feel confident is possible and I will work on that for 30 days and celebrate my progress.

9. **Self-pity and excuses**: I will take responsibility for my behavior. I will tune into the negative and blame-shifting inner conversations and neutralize them with positive affirmation – Yes, I can! Nothing can stand in my way.

10. **The pastry counter**: I am going to stay in the aisles where good food is and not even go there.

Now that you know what you want and have an action plan for overcoming your obstacles, it's time to take action.

KEEP YOUR HEAD IN THE GAME

The more visual reminders, the more written insights, the more voices cheering you on, the more likely you are to succeed. Here are some things you can do to keep your head in the game.

Post Pictures Take a before picture. Okay, you can put your clothes back on now. Also, find a photo of you looking healthy and fit. If you don't have one, find an inspirational magazine photo of someone with your basic body type and age who looks fit. Post these where you can see them daily.

Invest in a journal
A recent study published in the *American Journal of Preventative Medicine* found that people who keep a food journal **lose twice the weight** of those who rely on diet and exercise alone.

Journaling brings light to the journey and will help you self-monitor. One of my clients, a nurse, said that when she began journaling she realized that she wasn't eating a few candies at the nurses' station as she passed, she was eating 20 pieces of candy a day. This amounted to roughly 15 teaspoons of added sugar a day.

Don't just journal the foods you eat and the exercise you get, also journal your feelings, moods and energy level. Here's an example of my journaled thoughts. The idea is just to process your thoughts and discover new things about yourself, as a result:

> *I messed up when I binged on Starbuck's Caramel Macchiatos last week for 2 days in a row, but I'm back on track. I have been realizing that when I'm not getting enough sleep, I have more of a tendency to want high-sugar breakfasts and LOTS of caffeine. When I have a high-sugar breakfast then I eat high-sugar for the rest of the day. So, I need to make sure I get enough sleep and a low-glycemic, balanced breakfast. I'm going to make a list of healthy breakfast foods before I go to the grocery store next Monday and get the same breakfast foods every week to help me stay on track. I am not getting a lot of support from my spouse, so I've been listening to motivational CDs in the car, on my way to work, to keep me encouraged. I realize I won't be perfect, but that's okay. I'm looking for progress, not perfection. I am just feeling better, more confident and secure. What a relief to see that my efforts are not in vain. Little changes are becoming big changes in regards to how I feel. I have A LOT more energy and my mood just seems lighter. Interesting.*

Read/Listen/Watch encouraging information
Expose yourself to supportive research and inspiring images of wellness. Watch a wellness show, pick up a health-oriented magazine or subscribe to a wellness blog. This will encourage you to stay the course. It will create a sense of being connected to others on a common journey and remind you of what is at stake if you don't stay on track.

Remember, do not compare yourself to others; but use others as healthy role models. You will always be you, but you can gain inspiration and wisdom from the examples of others.

Find an accountability partner
Accountability is one of the most important factors in staying on track with your health and fitness goals. When you have to report to someone else you feel pressure to perform.

Find a friend who wants to make some lifestyle changes too, and report to each other daily. No doubt, there is someone at church, at work, in your book club, your community or support group who would be willing to be an accountability partner.

Find a coach
Sometimes that third party who keeps you on track and pushes you to break through your limitations can make all the difference in the world.

For resources to help you stay on track with your goal to GET OFF YOUR BUTT visit www.lydiamartinez.com.

Beverly Pinske

Novelist

My saga began in 2007. Bonnie Church, a friend and wellness columnist for a regional women's magazine, approached me to take part in an experiment. She said if I consistently followed Coach Lydia's' and her instruction for 12 weeks, she was confident I could reduce my size and improve my health, perhaps dramatically. She insisted that I keep my physician in the loop so he could track my progress.

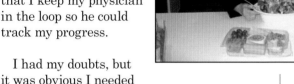

I had my doubts, but it was obvious I needed to do something. At that time I was taking lots of medication for diabetes and blood pressure. I lived on pain pills by day and sleeping pills by night. I needed a motorized cart and wheelchair to get around.

I was aware of how unhealthy I had become and I knew what that meant. I had recently lost both my mom and dad. Mortality was very real.

Though I was wearing a size 20 at the time, I was not that interested in losing weight. I had done that before—only to gain it all back plus some. I just wanted to get off some of my medication and feel like a vibrant, living human being again. So, I said "yes" to the experiment, but secretly thought, "This is going to be a very long 12 weeks!!"

Well, I was wrong. To my surprise, within 8 weeks I went from a size 20 to a size 14. I was ecstatic. I dramatically reduced my medication. I no longer had to rely on pain pills to get through the day, or sleep aids to get through the night. My doctor was thrilled.

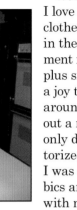

Wow! This was fun. I love shopping for clothes, particularly in the misses department rather than the plus size division. What a joy to be able to walk around the mall without a mobility aid. I not only didn't need the motorized cart any more, I was doing water aerobics and taking walks with my husband, Glen in the beautiful NC Mountains where we live.

Glen was supportive and so very proud of me. We were both so impressed with the transformation that I decided to become a TLS Coach [TLS Weight Loss Solution is the wellness program Bonnie and Lydia used to help me]. Glen was going to help me develop my business. There is no better way to make a living than helping people get healthy so they can live a full life. We both looked forward to creating income together to fund our retirement.

Tragically, I lost my husband to cancer within a year. This is a sadness only those who have walked through that valley can understand. I don't know if I could have survived it if I had not gotten well. Living my new lifestyle, I had the energy I needed to care for Glen in his final days.

The disciplines I learned helped equip me for widowhood. I had learned that victory comes through a series of daily choices. I was tempted to crawl into a hole, grieve, eat comfort foods and revert back to my old habits. Though I had days like that, I knew how to get back on track - one meal at a time, one snack at a time and one walk at a time.

In 2010, I needed a hip replacement. Years of obesity and sedentary living had irreparably damaged the joint. My surgeon was quite clear that the surgery would not have been possible had I not lost all that weight and had my diabetes under control. The operation was a great success and I'm feeling wonderful.

Though I miss Glen, I have not allowed widowhood to slow me down. I recently published my first novel "Pawns of Deception". The basic principles of wellness - Low glycemic-centered eating, exercise, managing stress - have continued to enhance the mental focus I need to write my books, the energy I need for my promotional tours and the self-confidence I need to meet the public at my book signings.

I live an abundant life, filled with purpose. Though God knows the number of our days, He lets me choose the quality of those days – one day at a time.

Tamara Adell

Featured on Biggest Loser

I married my high school sweetheart in the 80's. It was an inter-racial marriage. In the south, during the 80s that was not socially acceptable.

People could be cruel. One night someone came and burned a cross in our yard as a demonstration of their disapproval. Perhaps our marriage could have survived that, but to make matters worse, my husband had several affairs with other women. He was also physically and verbally abusive to me and the children.

Life together was difficult, but it got worse when we went through the trauma of having our daughter violently murdered. The case remains unsolved to this day. Around that same time, I was diagnosed with cancer. [I am grateful to say, that I am now cancer-free].

Not unlike many women who live with domestic abuse, I continued to hope that he would change, but his abuse escalated. One day he beat me and threatened to kill me. I ended up in a domestic violence shelter. We are now divorced.

That was a turning point for me. I had been angry with God for taking my daughter, for not 'fixing' my husband and for the cancer that weakened me. I began to understand that this was not God's plan for my life. His plan was to give me an abundant purposeful life. He was not to blame for my husband's abuse or my daughter's murder, or my cancer.

I asked for forgiveness and entrusted myself to His care.

Since then, life has changed dramatically. I have learned to trust God and cultivate the character I need to live life fully.

I became increasingly aware that I needed to lose weight. I was 5'4" and 262 lbs.. I was destroying one of the most beautiful gifts that God had given me, my body.

I had struggled with weight loss all my life. As the oldest child of four, My sisters were cute and petite and my brother was slim and I was 'the big one'. That was my identity. I just accepted that I was going to be a heavy person for the rest of my life.

The idea of starting "a diet" was not on my radar. I had tried that before only to gain my weight back. But they were offering a weight loss program at my job, and they needed a 4th person to participate.

This decision to participate launched me into a major lifestyle change.

- I began to journal everything I was eating. And I don't cheat. If it goes into my mouth, I write it down.
- I eliminated gluten and sugar from my diet.
- I learned how to read labels.
- I began exercising regularly. I started out with a stationary foot pedal that I

kept under my desk at work. I would pedal away throughout the day.
- I joined a fitness center and hired a trainer.

I was determined to lose 100 lbs.. It is now 3 years later and I have lost 123 lbs.. I shrank from a sizc 24 to a size 6. My success has been featured on the popular weight loss show, 'The Biggest Loser'.

The keys that have helped me to transition from a life of defeat to a life of victory include;

- I don't look back.

- I draw daily strength from the Lord to handle what this day brings.
- I have a strong reason why. I want to be here for my son, and now my infant grandson.
- I keep it simple. Losing weight and living well is just a matter of replacing bad habits, with good habits.

I am very excited about my new career as TLS Weight loss Solution Coach. Through this system I will be equipping others with the tools they need for a lifetime of wellness.

PART 3

7 STEPS TO GETTING OUT OF YOUR RUT

GET OUT OF YOUR RUT

Some of the most powerful moments of our life occur when we are feeling 'stuck'. The pain of being stuck is the fuel that drives us to step out of our ruts and search for different ways of doing things.

This section focuses on 7 common ruts that might be impeding your progress toward you goals. A rut is a 'way of doing things' that works against you, but you keep doing it anyway. It's the behavior that is keeping you 'stuck.' It's the bad habit that needs to be broken.

I understand ruts. I was deeply embedded in one for a good portion of my life. I had bad habits and misguided ideas that could have destroyed me. If I had not chosen to break those habits and change my attitude, my rut would have eventually become my grave. Like they say, a rut is merely a grave with the ends knocked out.

The tough part is this:

To get out of your rut, you first have to admit you are in one.

This requires the painful light of truth. You have to see and admit your imperfections. You have to think through the consequences your behavior is having on others and on yourself. It can be painful to be exposed. But there is no other way.

One of the reasons we resist self-evaluation is we live in an era that esteems denial. We are led to believe "If I think positively, if I pretend that I don't have issues, then I don't have issues."

If you convince yourself you don't have a problem, you won't seek a solution.

- If you kid yourself into believing you are in better physical shape than you are, you will not focus on improving your fitness.

- If you kid yourself into believing a line of credit is the same thing as wealth, you will bury yourself into the rut of debt.

- If you blame peoples negative reaction to you as 'their problem, not mine' you will never deal with your relationship-wrecking behaviors.

Getting really honest about who you are – the lovely and the ugly – is the first step to making a change

So, let's get honest.

Now I don't mean pessimistic. You should feel incredible HOPE. Your rut is the result of repeating unhealthy behaviors over and over again. Replace those destructive behaviors with constructive behaviors and you bust the rut.

There are many habits that could have been addressed in this section. This section addresses some of the most common ruts related to — relationships, mental attitude, time management and finances.

- Look through the table of contents and choose the bad habit that is most pressing; the one that is creating the most pain in your life. Focus there.

- Make a 30 day commitment to the recommended action steps. Some habits can be broken in a few days, some take months; but if you are committed to cultivating new behaviors, you will make progress.

If you need the assistance of a wellness or life coach to keep you on track during the process of change, find one. Consider it an investment in yourself — one of the most important investments you can make.

For additional resources to help you bust your ruts visit lydiamartinez.com.

RUT ONE:

NEGATIVE SELF TALK

Your self-image is your opinion of who you are and what
you think you can or cannot achieve. We begin forming
these opinions the moment we spring from the womb. The
media, society, authority figures, friends and family begin
to tell us who we are and if we make 'the cut' in the areas of
beauty, intelligence and talent.

Thoughts in your mind are like cables. They can strengthen and support or shackle your life. - Dennis Waitley

Your self-image is your opinion of who you are and what you think you can or cannot achieve. We begin forming these opinions the moment we spring from the womb. The media, society, authority figures, friends and family begin to tell us who we are and if we make 'the cut' in the areas of beauty, intelligence and talent.

As children, we have no choice but to absorb these opinions. They are 'reality' as far as we are concerned. If these influential people have a definition of 'success, beauty and talent' that is inconsistent with who we are, our self-image is affected. We begin to tell ourselves, "If that is what success, beauty and talent look like; I am definitely not successful, attractive, smart, nor talented."

We get into the rut of basing our worth on other people's opinions of us and dig it deeper with our words – both the words in our head and the words on our tongue.

WORDS AFFECT US PHYSICALLY

The software (thoughts) will run the hardware (mind and body). - Dennis Waitley

In his book, "How to Win the Battle of the Tongue," Morris Cerrulo notes that neurosurgeons discovered that the speech center of the brain has dominion over the nerve center of the body. Speech has so much power that simply 'speaking' can trigger feelings and inspire action. Some examples:

- If you were to repeatedly say, "I'm feeling weak," then your nerves would relay that message to your body and you would begin to feel weak. In natural sequence, your body would adjust to a physical attitude of weakness.

- If you were to say, "I have no ability. I can't do this job," Guess what? You limit your ability to do that job to your full potential. The central nervous system 'gets the message' that you are not able. You will feel like giving up.

- If you keep saying, "I'm so fat and tired," then the body responds, "Yes, you are fat and you are tired". It then prepares to live up to those words and take actions that will contribute to the condition of being 'fat and tired'.

- If you keep saying, "I am poor," then you will condition yourself to attract poverty. You will feel at home in poverty. It will feel more comfortable to 'be poor' and you will self-sabotage your efforts to change that condition.

- On the other hand, if you say, "I am capable! I am energetic! I can achieve success!" Then your whole body will be magnetized toward success and energy. You'll be ready to meet any challenge and ready to conquer the obstacles to your success.

Bottom line: What you speak, that's what you're going to get.

HOW TO CHANGE THE CONVERSATIONS IN YOUR HEAD

Pleasant words are like a honeycomb, sweetness to the soul
and health to the bones. (Proverbs 16:24)

Negative self-talk can be described as those indictments that you dump on yourself continually. They are the things that you say to yourself, but would never even consider saying to someone else. They can destroy you. That is why it is important to affirm yourself with words that speak success and not failure.

Negative Self-Talk

STEP ONE: TUNE IN TO THE VOICES

In order to change your 'negative head talk' you need to realize it is going on. There are 3 primary types of negativity.

1. "I AM NOT' statements

"I'm not worthy."
"I'm not capable."
"I'm not talented."
"I'm not going to succeed."
"I'm not [fill in some positive attribute]."

Note: An 'I AM NOT!' statement is not the same thing as a sober assessment of who you are and who you aren't. A sober assessment can actually help you clarify your goals and expectations. The famous Serenity Prayer should be on all of our tongues - "Help me to change [improve] the things I can. Help me to accept the things I cannot change [improve] and give me the wisdom to know the difference." In contrast, 'I AM NOT' statements are based on warped perceptions, not reality.

2. Punishing statements

When you do something that you wish you hadn't, punishing statements rake you over the coals, over and over again.

> *"You are such a loser."*
> *"I can't believe you ate that piece of cake."*
> *"I can't believe you had that fender bender."*
> *"You are a lazy slob. Face it!"*

3. 'Woe is me' statements

Self-pity is fueled by those unending whining laments about YOU.

"But, Lydia, you don't understand. Nothing ever works out for me. Things are always against me. I just can't seem to win." Waa. Waa. Waaaa.

These 3 types of negative statements stand in the way of your progress. They can powerfully alter your life. For example:

- If you convince yourself through your thoughts and words that you will always be fat, you will not be motivated to change your diet and lifestyle habits.

- If you convince yourself through your thoughts and words that you will always be poor, that poverty is your lot in life; you will not be motivated to dream big and move toward your goals.

- If you convince yourself through your thoughts and words that there is 'no way' out of your rut, you will give up trying.

Your vision of yourself becomes a self-fulfilling prophecy.

STEP TWO: VISUALIZE THE PERSON YOU ARE BECOMING

Just like getting the crap out of your kitchen and stocking your shelves with good stuff; you need to get the crap out of your head and the good stuff in.

Ask yourself:
What does it look like to be…

- Off my butt

  Example: Size 8, energetically walking with head held high.

- Out of my rut

  Example: Opening up a fridge filled with colorful fruits and veggies. Grabbing my mp3 for a walk with the dog in the park. Countering negative judgments about others with positive reflections.

- On with my life

  Example: Sitting on the Board of Directors for the Community Arts Council. Taking a medical mission trip each year. Eating good food on the deck of my ocean-side condo with my family.

> ***Instead of "I don't worry" say "I am confident".***
>
> ***Instead of "I will become secure" say "I am secure".***

That image is your mental and emotional GPS, moving you in the direction of your goals.

STEP THREE: CREATE 'I AM' STATEMENTS CONSISTENT WITH THAT IMAGE

'I AM' statements are NOT a magic wand binding God to act on your behalf. These statements are your inner cheerleader, reminding you of what is possible and motivating you to stay on track.

'I AM' statements are spoken in the present tense. They reflect a healthy self-image. They are stated 'in the positive' rather than 'in the negative'.

- Instead of "I don't worry" say "I am confident".
- Instead of "I will become secure" say "I am secure".

Examples:

- *I am a good person. I have integrity. I do what is ethically right and good.*

- *I am stronger, wiser, and more tolerant. I am strong enough to understand and make allowances for other people's weaknesses, and their behavior towards me. Other people's behavior is about them, not me.*

- *I focus on the joy of living my life and helping others where and when I can.*

- *I am what I eat and drink, so I eat and drink good things.*

- *I exercise, which I enjoy. I walk when I don't need to drive or take the bus or train.*

- *I smile and laugh whenever I can - life is good. Getting caught in the rain reminds me that it is good to be alive to feel it.*

- *I forgive other people. Deep down everyone is a good person, just like me. I am a compassionate, loving, and caring person.*

I AM ...you fill in the blanks.

STEP FOUR: CONTINUALLY REWIRE YOUR THOUGHTS

The next time you hear negative chatter in your head – stop it abruptly. Say out loud, "I cancel that" and instantly substitute a positive and powerfully encouraging thought. If you are in a place that you can't speak out loud, wear a rubber band on your wrist and snap it - and redirect your thinking to an empowering thought.

As we change our inner (voice) chatter, we literally rewire our brains. Negative self-talk repeated over and over hardwires self-doubt and discouragement. Positive self-talk repeated over and over hardwires confidence and positive expectation. Interrupting negative talk and replacing it with positive talk will hardwire your brain to be a partner with you in reaching your goals.

The good news is that the brain is capable of rewiring itself no matter how old you are.

STEP FIVE: BE GRATEFUL

Gratitude transforms you. Psychologists have found that practicing gratitude actually improves the health of your mind and your body. You have much to be thankful for. God has given you many gifts.

PURPOSE: A reason for living.
TIME: To fulfill your purpose.
PERSONALITY: The essence of YOU.
A BODY: A way to get you where you want to go.
RESOURCES: To sow and reap.

Be grateful!

"If ever there is tomorrow when we're not together - there is something you must always remember. You are braver than you believe, stronger than you seem, and smarter than you think." Christopher Robin said to Pooh

RUT TWO:

GOSSIP AND JUDGEMENT

The tendency to judge people over and over again with
your tongue is the fruit of being unforgiving.
Human beings are imperfect [and that includes you]. When
you truly embrace that fact, and learn to forgive, you will
be less judgmental and more compassionate. It will be
reflected in how you talk about others.

We are all guilty of talking trash about people.

There ARE times to discuss ugly realities with a trusted friend or counselor. That is not what I mean. I mean gossip [malicious talk] and judgment [malicious opinions]. However you label it, talking trash serves no good purpose.

Gossip comes in many seemingly innocent disguises.

- **The "I heard..."or "They say that..." technique**: This allows the gossip to protect the 'source' and deflects guilt from the gossiper. After all, it wasn't 'ME' who said it.

- **The sandwich technique**: A positive statement is made about someone, which is then followed by a long list of negatives. "Yes, she's a sweet girl, BUT isn't it a pity that she…" The next 10 minutes are spent ripping her to shreds. By this method, one can appear sympathetic to the person they are gossiping about.

- **The pseudo-spiritual technique**: Spiritualized gossip might be the worst gossip of all. It sounds something like this: "Jane needs our prayers…" followed by a total analysis of Jane's weaknesses so that others can pray more 'intelligently' for her.

Why do we do this?

Hurting people, hurt people. - John Maxwell

Connection Humans have a strong desire to connect with others. It is in our DNA. Unfortunately, we sometimes seek out negative ways to connect. A mutually shared, negative opinion about another human being is an easy way to connect. This is a perverted bond, but it is a connection, and we like to connect.

Elevation When we feel insecure about who we are, we belittle others. This takes the focus off of our shortcomings and puts it on the weaknesses of others. Another way to 'elevate' ourselves is to seek out the company of other insecure people. We can then gang up and gossip about the confident people of the world.

Vindication When offended, we seek revenge. We punish our offenders by reciting their offenses to anyone who will listen. In a court of law, a defendant can only be judged once for a crime committed. When we do not forgive, it is like declaring someone guilty and trying them in the courtroom of our mind – over and over and over again.

Addiction Emotional 'drama' triggers our body to produce adrenaline. Adrenaline is like a bio-chemical morphine. When we are constantly preoccupied with other people's lives, we remain in a state of vexation. When vexed, adrenaline is triggered and we get a high. This creates addiction.

Compensation for the past Sometimes we try to compensate for pain in the past. The kid who was teased and bullied becomes the adult who teases and bullies.

What is the outcome of gossip and negative talk about others?

Gossip and Judgements

- Just like poison ivy, the more you scratch it, the more it itches. The momentary satisfaction you feel after scratching that itch to gossip is short.
- You lose posture and beauty.
- Gossip becomes part of your identity and it repels people. It's like verbal flatulence.
- You run the risk of bringing anger and bitterness into every relationship and new experience.
- Your life can become so wrapped up in what's wrong with everyone else that you can't enjoy others.
- Constantly judging siphons off the energy you need to focus on your goals.
- You will begin to feel that your life lacks meaning or purpose.
- You will feel at odds with your spiritual beliefs.
- You will lose valuable and enriching connections with others.
- Your emotional health will be affected by depression, a hot temper, anxiety and emotional pain. This, then, takes the physical form of headaches, backaches, fatigue and stress. Stress destroys the immune system.
- If you are unforgiving and judgmental toward others, you will be unforgiving and judgmental of yourself.

Do you feel like eating worms - GOOD! Irritation is a powerful motivation for change. Instead of eating worms, take action.

How can you break this habit?

- Forgive yourself.
- Forgive others.

The tendency to judge people over and over again with your tongue is the fruit of being unforgiving. Human beings are imperfect [and that includes you]. When you truly embrace that fact, and learn to forgive, you will be less judgmental and more compassionate. It will be reflected in how you talk about others.

 know from personal experience how powerful forgiveness is. I have to work through the act of forgiveness on a regular basis. When I surrender my judgments and choose to forgive, my attitude changes. I begin to respond to others with understanding, kindness and respect.

Forgiving an offense does not mean forgetting an offense. Old situations still pop into my head and can potentially trigger negative thoughts [judgments] and negative talk [gossip]. The difference is, as I practice forgiving others, I get better at it and can recover quickly. So will you.

STEP ONE: Write down the offenses that keep you 'stuck' in the spiral of judgments [indictments] and gossip [trash talk].

- *What have others said to you that hurt you?*
- *What have others done to you that damaged you?*
- *What have you done that you can't forgive yourself for?*
- *What attitudes and resentments are holding you back from being the productive, positive and energetic person you long to be?*

STEP TWO: List the people in your life that you need to forgive.
[Start with at least 3].

A good indication that you need to forgive someone is when the offense keeps gnawing at you. Perhaps you find yourself feeling happy when you hear some bad news about the offender and you can't wait to share the bad news with someone.

- *Who are they?*
- *How did they offend or hurt you?*
- *How will life improve if you 'forgive' them and are no longer held prisoner by the negative emotions and behavior that accompany judgments and lack of forgiveness?*

STEP THREE: Write an honest account of the offense.

To experience the cleansing and purification of forgiveness you must recount the emotions that were triggered as a result of the offense. Your account can be a couple paragraphs or several pages. Describe how you felt– the pain, the guilt, the rage, the shame. You no longer have to hold on to it.

STEP FOUR: Share your account with someone you trust.

This brings the offense into the light. When brought into the light, its power over you diminishes.

STEP FIVE: Forgive your offender.

> "The weak can never forgive. Forgiveness is the attribute of the strong."
> -Mahatma Gandhi

Forgiveness is a gift you give to yourself. It is not something you do for someone else.

Forgiveness means you will no longer waste your energy thinking about the offense. You will no longer diminish your dignity by gossiping about the offender.

STEP SIX: Forgive yourself.

You are an imperfect human. You 'screw up' too. Forgiveness does not mean ignoring your poor judgment or the mistakes you have made. It is acknowledging your errors then releasing yourself from ongoing judgment. Forgiveness is giving yourself a clean slate to start again.

> **Forgiveness does not mean ignoring your poor judgment or the mistakes you have made. It is acknowledging your errors then releasing yourself from ongoing judgment.**

STEP SEVEN: Enjoy the benefits.

There are numerous studies that show the mere act and intention of forgiveness can improve your well-being. Some of the benefits are:

- Healthier relationships
- Increased energy
- Emotional stability
- Decreased risk for disease
- Richer spiritual life
- Less stress and hostility
- Lower blood pressure
- Reduced symptoms of depression, anxiety and chronic pain
- Lower risk of alcohol and substance abuse

"To forgive is to set a prisoner free and discover that the prisoner was you."
    - Lewis B. Smedes, "Forgiveness - The Power to Change the Past"

RUT THREE:

OUT OF CONTROL EATING

Overeating creates more pain than it resolves.
It sabotages your self-esteem, your energy levels and the
length of your life.
Despite the pain, you keep shoveling it in. Why?

WARNING: If over [or under]eating is out of control to the point of creating physical illness or unhealthy behaviors, [such as binge and purge, or regularly eating to the point of physical pain] please seek out professional help. You are worth it.

Overeating creates more pain than it resolves.

- Gas and bloating
- Fatigue
- Mood swings
- Fat gut and butt
- Shame

It sabotages your self-esteem, your energy levels and the length of your life. Despite the pain, you keep shoveling it in. Why?

Let's explore the factors that influence the tendency to overeat.

- **Hormonal Imbalances**: My minds says, NO! My body says, NOW!
- **Food cravings**: Mmm. A bag of potato chips sounds really good right now.
- **Emotional Eating**: I'm stressed. Pass me the chocolate chip cookies.
- **Mindless Eating**: Silently transfixed by the TV, bowl of ice cream in hand.

HORMONE-BALANCING TIPS

The foundation of getting out of the overeating rut is to normalize two sensations:

- Hunger [I need to eat!]
- Satiety [I need to stop eating!].

These sensations are in part controlled by two hormones: Grehlin [triggers the desire to eat] and Leptin [tells the body it has had enough].

Hunger: The physical sensation that you need to eat.

Think about the rumbling in your stomach. That's a physical sensation telling you that you are hungry. That sensation of hunger is due to the presence of a hormone call 'grehlin'. Grehlin is the "Hey, I'm hungry when do we eat?" hormone.

Your stomach makes ghrelin when it's empty. It slows the production of grehlin when it's full. If you want to stop overeating, you want to produce less ghrelin. Some steps that you can take to normalize your grehlin levels are:

TIP ONE: Get enough sleep – 7-9 hours a night. Sleep deprivation elevates grehlin.

TIP TWO: Eat every 3-4 hours. Starvation triggers grehlin.

Satiety: The condition of physically feeling full

"A sense of being full", turns off hunger. This is partly due to an elevation of a hormone produced by the fat cells called - leptin. Leptin tells your body that you have had enough, so stop eating, now!

Overeating

The more fat you have, the more leptin you make - so 'theoretically' the less food you'll eat. You would think that would be great news for those with a lot of fat on their body. Unfortunately, that is not how it works.

When you are overweight you become insensitive to leptin. Though there is plenty being produced, your body isn't listening. It is similar to insulin resistance. Insulin resistance occurs when there's lots of insulin being produced in response to a diet high in crappy carbs, but the body has stopped responding to the insulin.

Bottom line, excess body fat can screw up your appetite signals and actually make you hungrier.

TIP ONE: Reduce Stress Stress triggers fat storage and sugar craving.
TIP TWO: **Exercise** Exercise builds lean muscle, burns fat and lowers stress.
TIP THREE: **Eat balanced meals** Balance your blood sugar one meal and one snack at a time.

FOOD CRAVING TIPS

Cravings are not a bad thing. They can be your best teachers. The good news is cravings pass IF not indulged. Here are six tips to help you hold on 'til they pass.

TIP ONE: Avoid sugary meals. When you eat a high sugar meal you start the roller coaster effect. The sugar spikes. This causes your pancreas to release insulin. What goes up, now, comes down. The blood sugar drops. Your body reacts to the sudden drop by releasing the stress hormone, cortisol. Cortisol triggers food cravings and fat storage.

The key to preventing this cycle is to satisfy your hunger with a healthy snack. Don't reach for that box of cookies. Reach for an energy boosting snack instead. How about some walnuts and an apple? It might not be your first choice at the moment, but it will help put the brakes on the roller coaster, and stop the dramatic rise and fall of your blood sugar.

> *Cravings are not a bad thing. They can be your best teachers. The good news is cravings pass IF not indulged. Here are six tips to help you hold on 'til they pass.*

TIP TWO: Drink plenty of water. Sometimes a craving for food is really a craving for water. Reach for a big glass of refreshing water before you reach for the sugary foods. This could take the edge off the craving and, even if you indulge, you probably won't indulge quite as much.

TIP THREE: Manage stress. We know what stress hormones do. They cause you to crave sugar and store fat. Before you snack, take some deep cleansing breaths and walk the dog for 10 minutes. Then come back and have a healthy snack.

TIP FOUR: Get a good night's sleep. If you don't get enough sleep at night, your hunger/satiety hormones will be out of whack. The result? You crave junk food but do not 'feel full' when you eat it. Go to bed before midnight and sleep 7-8 hours.

TIP FIVE: Eat enough. Remember if you let your blood sugar get too low, it will trigger that craving for sweets. This is because your body wants to bring that sugar back up as quickly as possible, and nothing does it like double chocolate New York cheesecake.

TIP SIX: Form new behaviors. Years ago there was a psychologist named Pavlov. He did an interesting experiment. He would ring a bell every time he fed a dog. After a while, the dog was so used to getting food when the bell rang, his mouth watered just at the sound of the bell.

If you grab a bag of chips and flop down on the couch to watch TV every day after work– your mouth will begin to water as you enter the door. You will mindlessly head for the chips in the cupboard.

Forming new habits will take the edge off this response. When you come home from work, instead of grabbing the chips and flopping down in front of the 'tube', do something else: Walk the dog for 15 minutes, gulp down a glass of water and have a handful of walnuts. Over time, you will cultivate new habits.

EMOTIONAL EATING TIPS

Food is intended to be fuel for your body, not a crutch for your wounded emotions. There is a difference between emotional eating and healthy eating.

- Emotional cravings for specific foods come on quickly and are just as quickly satisfied.
- Healthy hunger creeps up gradually and then goes away gradually as you eat.

TIP ONE: Don't Pull the Trigger. Identify your trigger foods and trigger emotions. A trigger food, sometimes called a 'comfort food', is a food that is craved due to emotion and not because of genuine hunger. These are the foods that can get you in the 'overeating' rut.

- Identify the emotions that cause you to reach for these foods - stress, depression, anxiety, or boredom? These are your trigger emotions.

- Identify the foods that you associate with pleasant memories or relaxation. Which foods cheer you up or reward you for good behavior? These are your trigger foods.

Trigger foods in the presence of trigger emotions is a recipe for overeating.

My three trigger foods are pizza, double stuffed Oreo™ cookies and carrot cake. Under times of stress, I would feel like I 'needed' Oreo™ cookies. I could suck down a sleeve of them in one sitting and then reach for another. I literally couldn't control myself.

There is a physical reason for that. Foods high in fat and sugar make the brain release "endogenous opioids" – biological morphine. Just like an addict is easily reminded of their drug, your brain's orbitofrontal cortex, the center of motivation and cravings, is stimulated when you taste (or even see or smell) foods you crave. So, if at times you feel that you are actually addicted to a certain food, you're right! You're getting high on that food.

Bottom line: When you feel that trigger emotion, do not reach for food. Don't pull the trigger. You need to comfort yourself with something other than food.

TIP TWO: Clean out the cupboards. Don't try to control with self-discipline what you can control with environment. In other words, if the Oreo's™ aren't in the cupboard, you won't be able to reach for them. The mere act of having to go somewhere to satisfy your craving gives you time to make healthier choices.

Those tempting foods have a way of creeping back into our cupboards. Identify the foods that are causing you to stumble. If you can't resist them or eat them in moderation; if they control you rather then you controlling them - then toss them out!

TIP THREE: Be prepared with alternative activities. Walk, swim, do yoga, read a book - Do something other than eating. These alternative activities can lower the desire to reach for the trigger foods.

TIP FOUR: If you do give in- know when to STOP. Emotional eating does not mean you have to engage in a food orgy. If you are committed to having that cookie anyway - first eat a low glycemic snack [String cheese perhaps] and drink a glass of water. Then have 2 small cookies instead of 2 sleeves of cookies. Don't fall into the 'all or nothing' trap. A couple cookies, a glass of water and a 10 minute walk might be all you need to feel satisfied and bring you back to reality.

MINDLESS MUNCHING TIPS

You might be a mindless eater if:

- You grab a bag of chips and before you know it, you're reaching for the last crumbs in the bottom.
- You sometimes forget whether you have eaten or not.
- You 'inhale' your food.

TIP ONE: Don't sit in front of the TV or computer with food. Once eating is under way, the brain sends out a signal when fullness is approaching. If the mind is "multi-tasking" during eating, the signals that regulate food intake may not be received by the brain. If the brain does not receive certain messages that occur during eating, such as the sensation of taste, it may fail to register the event as "eating". This scenario can lead to the brain continuing to send out additional signals of hunger, increasing the risk of overeating.

TIP TWO: Slow down. Divide your food in half. Eat half of what is on your plate and wait 5 minutes before you eat the other half. This will give your body an opportunity to feel full. Once finished, do not eat any more food for at least 5 minutes. Lay down your eating utensil between bites and chew your food slowly. Try eating with chop sticks or the non-dominant hand.

TIP THREE: Savor your food. Don't dive in. When your food is brought to the table, look at your plate. Note the colors, textures and fragrance. Sensually savor the first bite of food. Chew it slowly and completely. Think about the flavor and texture. Observe how it feels in your mouth. Starting slowly will help set the pace for the entire meal.

IF YOU FALL BACK INTO THE RUT

Whatever your overeating challenge is, commit to an action plan for change –but expect failure. Wow, is that a negative affirmation? No. It is reality. None of us are perfect. The good news is, you don't have to be. Doing the right thing, **most of the time**, yields dramatic results.

If you temporarily fall back into the overeating rut - forgive yourself. Learn from your lapse. Identify what 'tripped you up' and take steps to 'head it off at the pass.'

Get back on track quickly! You make positive choices one meal and one snack at a time. Make your next meal or snack a healthy one.

RUT FOUR:

PROCRASTINATION

Procrastinators are often high potential underachievers
living a mediocre life. They never reach their potential
because they keep putting off doing the things that
enhance their life.

Are you one of those people who think 'someday' is actually a day of the week?

"Someday I am going to get fit."
"Someday I am going to start my own business."
"Someday I am going to learn Spanish."

You are not alone. Putting off something that needs [or we want] to get done afflicts many of us. It is called procrastination. You see procrastinators everywhere. They are sitting at their desks shuffling papers or on their couches mindlessly surfing the tube.

Procrastinators are often high potential underachievers living a mediocre life. They never reach their potential because they keep putting off doing the things that enhance their life:

- They are dissipating their wealth by not paying their bills on time and getting socked with late fees and penalties.
- They are squandering their talents by not taking the time to get the education they need to pursue an advanced profession.
- They are destroying their health by not sticking with a plan that will move them toward their fitness goals.

Does that sound like you? Beware. Procrastination is to your life what dessert is to your body. Too much, too often will EVENTUALLY destroy you.

In psychology, **procrastination** refers to the act of replacing high-priority actions or tasks with low-priority actions and thus putting off important tasks to a later time.

The reasons people put off doing high priority tasks are many, Do any of the following describe you?

- **Anxiety avoidance**: You dread the stress of starting and completing a task and, worse yet, completing it unsuccessfully.
- **Self-limiting belief**: You are mired in fatalistic thinking. I'm too old to start thinking about planning for retirement.
- **ADHD**: You have physiological issues such as Attention Deficit Hyperactivity Disorder [ADHD]. This cognitive malfunction makes it difficult to filter out distracting stimuli in order to stick with a task 'til completed. Someone afflicted by ADHD tends to run from one uncompleted task to another.
- **Depression**: You are stuck with a sense of hopelessness. This makes starting and maintaining focus on a task difficult.
- **Perfectionism**: You would rather not do something at all if you can't do it perfectly.
- **Poor time management**: You don't realistically assess the time required to complete a task and, thus, put it off 'til 15 minutes before it's due.

- **Lack of goals**: You have no clue what you want so you wander aimlessly through your day, week, year, and lifetime.
- **Pleasure seeking:** If it ain't fun, you ain't doing it.

I want to focus on a simple strategy that can help you overcome your procrastination habit.

IDENTIFY AND STICK TO YOUR PRIORITIES

Time is limited. You get 24 hours per day and 365 days per year. Once a minute has passed, it's gone forever. That is why it is important for you to carefully think about how you spend those valuable minutes.

The first step to effectively using your time is to establish your priorities. A priority is something that is important to you NOW that leads you to the fulfillment of your life goals LATER.

Procrastination

Once you establish what your priorities are, before committing to a request for help or an exciting opportunity, ask yourself: *Is this activity consistent with my priorities? Will this activity lead me toward my goal?* If you cannot answer "yes", then say NO!!!

ELIMINATE TIME WASTERS

Assess where you are now. What activities on your calendar are wasting your valuable time? Are you volunteering for activities that are inconsistent with your priorities because you are afraid to say NO? Are you jumping on opportunities to 'do fun stuff' because you want to avoid the tasks that are 'less fun' but more consistent with your goals and priorities?

Identify your time-wasters

- List the activities that you are currently engaged in that are getting your focus OFF your priorities *[Examples: television watching, running errands for a community group that does not reflect your priorities]*

Identify your goal-reaching activities

- List activities that are consistent with your priorities and will lead you toward your goals. *[Examples: working on a writing project, attending a chamber of commerce function, volunteering for a domestic violence shelter]*

Take Action

- Terminate the commitments that don't align with your priorities. Yes, this might mean getting the courage to call and resign from a community group.

- Replace low priority activities with high priority activities. Yes, you might have to endure the discomfort of running to your computer and writing rather than turning on the TV to veg-out.

The painful truth is this – if you say YES to the activities that do not lead you toward your goals, you are saying NO to the future achievements and experiences you really want.

LEARN TO SAY NO.

Perhaps you are a people pleaser and do not like to tell people NO. Or, perhaps, you are a person that doesn't want to miss a thing. You are complicating your life with energy draining, non-productive activities.

- **Before making a commitment, ask yourself:** Will this activity lead me closer to my goals? Remember, if you fill your life with time-wasters it siphons off your focus from the things that you want to do. If the commitment does not lead you closer to your goal, don't do it. It is as simple as that.

- **Give yourself a 24 hour 'cooling off' period** before responding to demands on your time. When someone asks you if you would be interested in baking 12 dozen cookies for the church bake sale, say, "I will get back with you tomorrow."

- **Negotiate a compromise.** Perhaps you are being asked to serve with an organization that aligns with your priorities, but you cannot commit much time for volunteer activities. Identify what you can realistically do without upsetting the balance in your life and offer to do that. For example, if you want to help with the church bake sale, but you don't have time to bake 12 dozen cookies, offer to contribute a couple boxes of store-bought cookies for the event.

- **Don't feel compelled to provide excuses.** Like Oprah says, "No, is a complete sentence." Say it with me, "NO!" You can say it with a smile, but that two letter word can turn you away from a life wasted to a life lived!

MANAGE YOUR TIME

STEP ONE: Make a 'To Do' list. Include on it everything that comes to mind that you need or want to accomplish. Larger goals will need to be broken down into smaller tasks.

Example:

LARGER GOAL: Get my certification as a weight coach.

TASK 1: Find a weight management certification training to attend.

STEP TWO: Categorize those tasks as:

Beware. Procrastination is to your life what dessert is to your body. Too much, too often will EVENTUALLY destroy you.

Do Now These are the most pressing tasks and need to be prioritized and done today.
Do Later These are tasks that are going to be scheduled in at a later time. This is strategic procrastination.
Delegate These are tasks that, if you have the funds or authority, you delegate to another. [Joe, Jr., help fold the laundry.]

STEP THREE: Determine the time necessary to complete tasks and schedule accordingly.

STEP FOUR: Schedule in goof off, veg-out, have fun time. We all need some down time. Just not to the point that it destroys our lives.

STEP FIVE: Before you go to bed each night, list the next day's urgent tasks. Schedule them in – and most importantly – DO THEM!

SCHEDULE YOUR ACTIVITIES AROUND YOUR ENERGY LEVELS

We each have a unique weather system that surrounds us like a bubble. Depending on the weather, we can feel energetic or in a slump; we can be tense or relaxed, bubbly and outgoing or detached and melancholy. That weather is affected by the food we feed our minds and bodies, if and how much we exercise, and how deeply we sleep. So, the first step in controlling the weather is to treat your body and mind well. [The 'how to's' of treating your body and mind well are outlined in GET OFF YOUR BUTT.]

But each of us also has a unique rhythm that is part of who we are. It's called the circadian rhythm. This rhythm regulates our cycles of wakefulness and sleepiness, mental clarity and brain fog, energy and fatigue throughout the day.

You might be a MORNING PERSON. You jump out of the bed, full tilt, and ready to seize the day. You have the most energy and mental focus first thing in the morning.

You might be a MID-MORNING or EVENING PERSON. Your energy kicks in after breakfast or in the evening.

So, why is it important to know this?

Organize your life, as much as you can, around your rhythms. When you put together your to-do lists, as much as you have control of your time, factor that in.

If you are a morning person, don't drain that high octane energy into mowing the lawn. Use that time to write the book you have been wanting to write or to meet with that hot prospect who is interested in your business idea. Save the mindless activities like cleaning out your email box, folding laundry or watching the tube for those brain dead moments.

Yes, I know, many of you reading this book don't have the luxury of organizing your activities around your rhythms. For all of us, there are times we have to be ON when we feel like being OFF. That is why this book begins with GETTING OFF YOUR BUTT. Living well will help you rise to those occasions.

Being mindful of your rhythms will help you control the things you are able to control much more effectively.

RUT FIVE:

ENSLAVING DEBT

There is a difference between needs and wants
Need- Something I have to have to survive.
Those things are few.

Want -Something I would like to have
and the sooner the better.

I am not a money expert, but I have had plenty of experience learning how to make money and manage it. If you are going to get out of debt there are a few things you need to understand.

There is a difference between needs and wants

Need- Something I have to have to survive. Those things are few.
Want -Something I would like to have and the sooner the better.

- Need - Shelter
  Want - Largest house in an upscale subdivision

- Need - Food and water
  Want - New York cheesecake with a double latte.

- Need - Transportation
  Want - Brand new silver Jaguar

- Need - Clothing
  Want - Italian leather platform ankle boots

If you are going to successfully get your spending under control, you must ask yourself a couple questions before making a purchase.

- Is this a need or a want?

- If this is a want, can I afford this NOW?

I am not suggesting you give up every pleasure, but if you are in debt, you will need to begin to reign in your spending. This might hurt a little, but trust me. The peace of mind that comes from getting out of debt, will bring far more pleasure, than the temporary pain of walking away from those platform ankle boots.

There is a difference between a debt and an investment.

Debt: Means you borrow money and pay back more than you borrowed through interest. By the time you finish paying off that debt, the items you went into debt for, cost you far more than they are worth.

Debt enslaves you. It limits your choices. It forces you to labor at a job that you might hate because you have to pay those mounting bills. It drains your energy and mental focus.

Investments: An investment means leveraging your money [and time] to create more prosperity in your life. When you invest, you do so with the expectation that this investment will eventually return more than it cost. Sound investments liberate you. They provide the money and time freedom required to enjoy life.

If you are in debt I have some good news! You can get out of this rut. It will require discipline and sacrifice, but you can do it.

Enslaving Debt

Debt-rut busting action plan

Step One: Become aware of your spending. Journal every penny you spend for at least two weeks and see where your money is going.

Step Two: Identify the money-wasters. Stop saying 'you are broke' when the truth is 'you are just wasting money.'

Take that cup o'Joe each morning. [I'm guilty!] If you spend $3 a day at a coffee bar [that is actually below what the average spends], you spend $1,095 a year on coffee. If you buy two cups - double that. That's $2000 + a year for your morning fix!

What about the green fuzzy food in your frig that you end up tossing at the end of the week? The average American throws away nearly $600 of wasted food each year. Twenty-nine million tons of food is wasted in the U.S. annually. That's enough to fill the Rose Bowl every three days!

Have you really calculated the high cost of eating fast food? If you eat one combo meal [burger, fries and drink] a day at @$4.50 this adds up to $1600 a year for food. But that does not include the potential health care costs associated with eating crap over a lifetime.

The National Business Group for Health estimates that the average total cost for a severe heart attack is about $1,000,000. That includes hospital charges, doctors, drugs, lost productivity and time away from work. Even if insurance picks up a large part of that bill, you are still going to pay thousands, one way or the other.

Step Three: Develop a budget. A budget establishes spending boundaries, so you do not spend more than you make. Here as some simple steps to creating a budget.

- **DETERMINE YOUR TOTAL INCOME**: Example: Job - $35,000 a year. Lawn business - $2000 a year. Add the amounts. This is your TOTAL INCOME.

- **DETERMINE YOUR FIXED EXPENSES**: Shelter, Car, Food, Toiletries [include savings] and the money you need to cover each expense. Add the amounts. This is your TOTAL FIXED EXPENSES.

This might hurt a little, but trust me. The peace of mind that comes from getting out of debt, will bring far more pleasure, than the temporary pain of walking away from those platform ankle boots.

SUBTRACT YOUR FIXED EXPENSES FROM YOUR INCOME: This is your DISCRETIONARY INCOME. The money left over for wants.

If you are consistently short on income to cover expenses, you need to either cut your spending or increase your income. We will talk more about ways to increase your income in the next section [Get On With Your Life].

Step 4: Develop a debt retirement plan.

- **Assess the damage.** Look at every one of your bills. See how much debt you owe, how much interest they charge on the debt and how much the minimum payment is. Add it up. This is your total debt.

- **Cut up the credit cards**. If your credit cards are creating temptation to purchase frivolous things, then get rid of them. Think about it. If you can't pay off your debt each month than you are paying interest on a steak dinner you ate last year or those shoes that have since been donated to the local thrift store.

- **Make payments on time**. Late fees can increase minimum payments and make it that much harder to pay off the debt. Do everything you can do to avoid these late fees. Pay your bill a week before the due date or set up online automatic payments to the credit card company a day or two before the due date.

- **Pay more than the minimum on all cards**. Paying the minimum can stretch out the amount of time you'll be paying off the cards. Try to pay at least $10-15 above the minimum on each card.

- **Consolidate your debt**. Take all your high interest individual debts and combine them into one low interest payment. Discuss your options with your bank or credit counselor.

- **Negotiate a lower rate**. 70% of Americans are living paycheck to paycheck; you are not alone in making this call. Don't let pride and fear cost you. Most companies are willing to negotiate rather than have you default on paying your credit card bill [or mortgage]. They are generally fair and reasonable. Even lowering the interest by a small percentage can make a big dent in your payments over time.

- **Request a credit report each year**. This will help you monitor and measure your progress. It will reinforce your commitment as you watch your debt liability shrink and your credit score will rise.

Step 5: If you don't know where to begin - get help!

- **Work with a credit counselor**: A credit counselor can help you identify some options for getting out of debt. Some will also talk to your creditors on your behalf.

- **Use debt management tools**: If you are going to manage this process on your own there are tools to help you do this listed in the recommended resource section of the book.

Yes, this is work - but it is worth it.

Imagine how great it will feel to indulge in your wants, without guilt. Imagine the freedom to make a generous contribution to your favorite charity without having to check your bank account first. Best of all, you will be cultivating the habits you need to create and manage the prosperity you were intended to have.

Trust me. Yes, one day the Italian leather ankles boots [or whatever!] can be yours.

RUT SIX:

ANNOYING PERSONALITY SYNDRONE

Before you leave the house, think about how you are going to 'behave' throughout the day. Looking good can enhance your personal attractiveness, but how you 'behave' is an even bigger factor in whether you attract or repel others.

Most of us take a look in the mirror before we leave the house. We want to make sure we are presentable. If there is spinach between our teeth, or our fly is down, we want to know it before walking out the door and meeting the world. Why? Because we are concerned about making a good impression on the people we meet.

I am going to ask you to take it one step further. Before you leave the house, think about how you are going to 'behave' throughout the day. Looking good can enhance your personal attractiveness, but how you 'behave' is an even bigger factor in whether you attract or repel others.

All of us, at least some of the time, annoy someone. We are all imperfect. We are all subject to moods and bouts of selfishness and insensitivity.   It is when our annoying tendencies begin to chronically interfere with our ability to make and sustain relationships that we are at risk.

The best barometer of whether we are annoying or attracting others is to observe how people respond to us. Ask yourself:

- Do people avoid me MOST OF THE TIME?
- Are they distracted when I talk to them MOST OF THE TIME?
- Do they cut off conversations with me MOST OF THE TIME?
- Do they 'change the subject' MOST OF THE TIME?
- Do they back away from me MOST OF THE TIME?

If you answer, "YES!" to those questions then you might have annoying personality syndrome.

Annoying behaviors that repel people, are just attractive behaviors gone bad. Sort of like a fresh loaf of bread turning green, fuzzy and fungal. When you open a fresh loaf of bread you go, "Ahhh." When you open a loaf that has gone bad you go, "Yuk."

For example

ATTRACTIVE PERSONALITY TRAIT: An energetic conversationalist

ANNOYING PERSONALITY TRAIT: Non-stop talking. This person is a motor mouth who won't let you get a word in edgewise. You find yourself lurching forward wanting to respond, but before you can, they have started rolling again. You are reduced to mono-syllables. "Uh, Eh, But…Bye-Bye."

ANNOYING PERSONALITY TRAIT: Always talking about themselves. This person likes to button hole you so they can recite their 'resume'. They can't wait to tell you the impressive things they are doing, the precocious things their kids are doing… Over and over again. You feel like saying, "I give up. Yes, you are awesome. Now get out of my face."

ATTRACTIVE PERSONALITY TRAIT: <u>Honest and straightforward.</u>

ANNOYING PERSONALITY TRAIT: Tactlessness. This person seems to delight in making people squirm. They say the right thing in the wrong way at the wrong time. Everybody is cringing like they are watching a train wreck about to happen.

ANNOYING PERSONALITY TRAIT: Advice-dispensing. You can't carry on a conversation with them without them offering advice on how you can fix that problem of yours. They are like a "What I would do if I were you… " vending machine.

Annoying Personality

ATTRACTIVE PERSONALITY TRAIT: <u>Humble and sensitive</u>

ANNOYING PERSONALITY TRAIT: Needy. They are constantly talking about the advantages everyone else has over them. Everyone else is better looking, smarter than them, whatever…. They continually fish for affirmation that they are 'okay'. And when you affirm them, they deflect it. "Oh, no-no. Not me."

ANNOYING PERSONALITY TRAIT: Overly apologetic. They have a hair-trigger "I'm sorry" button. You are riding with them in a car. You reach for your sweater and they start in," I'm sorry. I should have thought to turn off the air conditioning. How insensitive of me…" You feel the need to constantly reassure them, that all is fine. This gets old.

ATTRACTIVE PERSONALITY TRAIT: <u>Self-Confident and assertive</u>

ANNOYING PERSONALITY TRAIT: Always the diva. They pout if the world does not knit a piece of carpet every time their foot hits the ground. They constantly demand that others do what they want done.

ANNOYING PERSONALITY TRAIT: Space invaders. They get too close. They point too much. It's like they are near-sighted and have to get close enough to count the pores on your nose. Even ickier is if they rub up against you inappropriately. Back off.

ATTRACTIVE PERSONALITY TRAIT   : Observant and realistic

ANNOYING PERSONALITY TRAIT   : Doom-sayers. The world is going to hades in a hand basket. They walk into a room and the weather system changes from fair to cloudy.

ANNOYING PERSONALITY TRAIT   : Overly opinionated. These folks have a strong moral compass and it's pointing up their doo-pah [aka butt]. They always have an opinion and of course, it is the 'right' one. Listening to them is like listening to fingernails on a chalk board.

ATTRACTIVE PERSONALITY TRAIT   : Expressiveness and creativity

ANNOYING PERSONALITY TRAIT   : The Drama queen. This person over-emotionalizes everything that happens to them. It is like they are perpetually auditioning for the lead role in a tragedy.

ANNOYING PERSONALITY TRAIT   : They can't resist gossip. They are like the thug with stolen goods, beckoning from the shadows. "Psst. Hey you. I got the poop on 'so and so' and I am sure you are going to wanna hear this. "

ATTRACTIVE PERSONALITY TRAIT   : Passionate about a cause

ANNOYING PERSONALITY TRAIT   : Persistent to the point of pushiness. You feel like they have you in a half-nelson and the only way to extricate yourself is to say, "Yes."

ANNOYING PERSONALITY TRAIT   : Insincere. They manipulate you with flattery. They are a true friend, til you no longer have anything to offer them, and then you do not exist.

The good news is that you don't have to be annoying. You can choose to behave differently. The transformation from annoying to attractive begins with a few simple steps.

Step One: Admit you have a problem.

You can't engage in your own recovery till you admit that you have something you need to recover from. This is, by far, the hardest step for anyone.

Our annoying behaviours develop overtime. We are so habituated to responding a certain way, we are not able to see clearly what we are doing and how it is affecting others. If you are having trouble identifying your issues, talk to a friend or family member, who will be straight up with you.

Step Two: Identify your attractive and annoying tendencies.

We come into this world with a 'pre-disposition' – it is called temperament. You cannot change that; but you can make choices about how you respond to circumstances.

There are many theories of temperament types but most derive in part from the observations of temperaments described by a man named Galen over 2000 years ago. He is credited with coining the terms, Choleric, Sanguine, Phlegmatic and Melancholy.

How would you describe your temperament?

> **All of us, at least some of the time, annoy someone. We are all imperfect. We are all subject to moods and bouts of selfishness and insensitivity. It is when our annoying tendencies begin to chronically interfere with our ability to make and sustain relationships that we are at risk.**

PHLEGMATIC
Definition: Not easily roused to feeling or action.

Attractive Qualities
Accepting of others
Laid back
Excellent mediators
Good administrators
Dry, quick sense of humor
Peaceful
Quiet
Composed, thoughtful and deliberate
Observant

Annoying qualities
Fade quickly
Lack of ambition
Slow to act
Indecisive
Directionless [no goals]
Tend to be passive/aggressive

SANGUINE
Definition: Cheerfully optimistic, hopeful, or confident.

Attractive Qualities
Life of the party
Good Networker

Able to get people enthusiastic about issues
Entertaining and engaging
Communicative
Optimistic
Sensitive, compassionate and thoughtful
Make friends easily
Loyal

Annoying qualities

Overpromise and under-deliver
Often late
Easily bored
Inability to follow through with tasks
Shallow and superficial
Flirtatious
Does not like to be alone
Careless
Talk too much
Speak before they think

CHOLERIC
Definition: testy, impatient and touchy.

Attractive Qualities
Decisive
High aspirations
Good leader
Driven to get things done
Ambitious
Energetic
Charismatic
Attractive
Persistent

Annoying qualities
Cranky when people or circumstances do not cooperate
Overly dominant and intimidating
Stubborn
Overly opinionated
Considers others weak

MELANCHOLIC
Definition: Tends toward gloom and depression.

Attractive Qualities
Deep thinker
Organized
Weighs positives and negatives before making decisions
Creative
Independent
Excellent counselors
Trustworthy and genuine
Willing to make sacrifices

Annoying qualities
Gloomy and pessimistic
Suffer from paralysis of analysis
Tend to isolate themselves
Inclined to despair and cynicism
Prone to depression
Perfectionistic

You are probably thinking - "Hey I'm a little bit of all of them." Most of us are a stew of different temperament types. But, generally, we fall into one or two types.

No matter, what your temperament blend is, your attractiveness quotient goes up or down depending on how you behave. Respond from your strengths [attractive qualities] and you are more attractive. Respond from your weaknesses [annoying qualities] and you are potentially annoying.

So where do we go from here?

Step Three: Make a commitment to change.

It's one thing to recognize you have a problem and quite another to do something about it. Commit to making a change for the better. You might want to write your commitment down, and post it somewhere as a reminder.

"I am committed to developing the habit of acting in a manner that is pleasant to be around, rather than annoying and unpleasant. To do so, I will mindfully cultivate the strengths of my temperament, so that they will dominate in my interactions with others."

Step Four: Tune in.

Start watching yourself closely. Remember, you are in control of how you behave. You can make choices about how to respond in every situation. If you find yourself acting annoying – Stop, take a deep breath and change your behavior.

For example:

If you find yourself nailing someone to the wall, with constant talking – stop. Back off, breathe and ask them a question about themselves. Shut up and listen.

If you hear yourself sounding cranky and opinionated, interrupt your rant with a statement such as, "I know that there are different points of view on this issue," and then ask the person you are talking with, "What are your thoughts?"

If they don't have any, then change the subject. That is a good indicator that they aren't all that interested in prolonging the conversation. If they do have some thoughts, listen respectfully.

It will feel funny, at first, to make a different choice and people may give you weird looks when you do. After a while, however, you, and they, will get used to it.

Step Five: Progress Daily.

Make the transformation from annoying to attractive, one day at a time. If your tendency is that you respond negatively to everything, set a goal to be positive for one full day.

When you have successfully achieved that, set the goal to two days and so on and so forth until you have officially broken that habit.

Step Six : Get Help.

Sometimes our negative traits are so deeply rooted that we are unable to overcome them without some help. If this is the case for you, seek the advice of a coach or counselor who is trained to help you handle your particular situation.

The good news is, as you seek to understand yourself, and cultivate the best of 'who you are', it will affect everyone around you. Your relationships will become healthier, and life will be alot more fun.

RUT SEVEN:

COMMUNICATION BREAKDOWN

It is helpful to understand what is going on in the brain
when we are communicating with one another.
There is a radar in our head that is continually scanning
the environment for threats. If it perceives a threat, stress
hormones are triggered to prepare us to run or fight.

Life is about connecting. It is something we all long for. It is how God wired us. This powerful desire to connect is what has fueled the viral growth of social websites like Facebook. We want connection!

However, where there is connection there is potential for conflict. Conflict can derail us. It creates stress and drains our emotional energy reserves. When it becomes a pattern in our significant relationships, it can keep us from pursuing our life goals.

Conflict is usually the result of communication breakdown. It is helpful to understand what is going on in our brains when we are communicating with one another. There is a powerful radar in our heads that is continually scanning the environment for threats. If it perceives a threat, stress hormones are triggered to prepare us to run or fight.

> *Life is about connecting. It is something we all long for. It is how God wired us.*

Some subconscious threats we perceive are:

- *They are demeaning me.*
- *They are confusing me.*
- *They are threatening my freedom to choose.*
- *They are going to harm me in word or deed.*
- *They are being totally unfair.*

These threats can be real or imagined. It doesn't matter. When we feel threatened, we respond. Our responses to real or imagined threat potentially add fuel to the fire.

- *We raise our voice.*
- *We shut down.*
- *We shift blame. The reason I am like this, is because you [fill in the blank].*
- *We go into the 'YOU ALWAYS DO THIS!!!' mode.*
- *We magnify the offense and make it bigger than it is.*
- *Our goal becomes to WIN THE ARGUMENT rather than to cultivate understanding.*

These behaviors trigger a threat response in the person we are communicating with, and the vicious cycle begins.

The good news is, you can break the cycle. Though the emotional reaction to threats is powerful, you also have a voice of reason in your head that can help you defuse the tension by responding rationally and graciously. As you learn to respond differently to perceived threats, conflict can lead to deeper intimacy and insight. But before you respond you first have to listen. Sometimes our 'bad listening habits' are what creates the communication breakdown to begin with.

Do any of the following describe how you listen to others?

The Conversation Habits that break down communication

- The Fake Listener: They show all the signs of listening, eye contact, nodding, making the right noises, but in reality they are not hearing a thing that is being said.

- The Interrupter: They are always planning their response. They tend to make statements, rather than ask questions to clarify what the person is trying to say. They often jump in before the other has finished speaking.

- The Intellectual: They react to the logic behind what someone is saying, rather than respond to the emotional intent of the speaker.

Communication Breakdowns

- The 'It's about me' after all: They are looking for an opportunity to change the focus of the conversation to them.

- The Lawyer: They listen defensively, ready to rebut what the other is saying. They take delight in proving the other person wrong.

- The Problem Solver: They jump in with the quick solution to a problem rather than listening carefully to the other persons' concerns.

Ouch! If you found yourself in those descriptions, don't dismay. The secret to overcoming the bad habits is to cultivate the good.

The Conversation Habits that enhance communication

- Relax, breathe evenly and listen carefully.

- If something is said, that gets your emotional radar beeping, don't let that throw you. Instead, listen and make an effort to understand their position. Ask questions. Others will more likely be willing to listen if they feel heard.

- Stay focused on the moment. This is not the time to bring up offenses from the past. That will only cloud the issue and make a peaceful resolution less likely.

- Respond to criticism with an openness to learn. Look for the grain of truth. Sometimes correction is not rejection, it is direction. When we take it too personally, we miss the opportunity to gain insight into how our words and actions are affecting others. Ask - Where is the criticism coming from? Why was it given? Was it given out of personal hurt (hurting people hurt people) or was it given for my benefit? Is it constructive or destructive? Sometimes what you need to hear most is what you want to hear least. Take the high road.

- Admit you are wrong – when you are. It diffuses the situation, sets a good example, and shows maturity. It also often inspires the other person to respond in kind, leading you both closer to mutual understanding and a solution.

- Use "I" statements. "I understand how you feel. I feel frustrated when this happens." Remember that the radar in their head is scanning for threats. When you say things like, "YOU MESSED UP," this elevates the other person's stress hormones and gets them in fight or flight mode. "I" statements defuse the threat.

- If appropriate, physically touch the person in a non-threatening way. Keep in mind, this would be someone who you have some degree of intimacy with, not necessarily your boss or workmates.

- Change the scene. Sometimes, just moving into another room or taking a walk together can have a calming effect on raw emotions.

- Move to the side. This moves you out of their personal space.

- Don't fold your arms. This is a closed posture and communicates you are in a defensive mode.

- Don't point. Pointing can be perceived as accusation.

- Take time to cool off. If you feel yourself or the person you are speaking with is starting to become too emotionally driven for the conversation to be constructive, it's okay to take a break from the discussion until you both cool off. Sometimes good communication means knowing when to take a break.

- Remember the goal is not winning. The goal is understanding. Instead of trying to 'win' the argument, look for solutions that meet everybody's needs.

- Don't give up. If you both approach the situation with a willingness to see the other's point of view and find a solution, you can make progress and break the cycle of conflict. Unless it's time to give up on the relationship, don't give up on communication.

CAVEAT: If someone is communicating with you on this level consistently, and leaving you drained and discouraged, you might have to sever the relationship. [Yes, there are relationships that cannot be easily severed- i.e., parents and children or husbands and wives. If these patterns persist in these familial relationships, seek out a qualified relationship coach or therapist to help you navigate through the conflict.]

Michele Cooper

Competitive Figure Skater

Every time I travel from New York to Pennsylvania to visit my grandchildren, I encounter an enormous tunnel that cuts through Blue Mountain. Early settlers must have spent weeks or months going around that mountain, but, thanks to some incredible engineering, I can drive right through it. I always thought of that tunnel as a good metaphor for how I face my personal mountains: I simply start climbing, take the long road or get out my drill or blasting caps and bore through the middle.

Like many women, I've faced my share of mountains. However, no matter how big the obstacle – addiction, job losses, failed marriages, single parenting, caring for a dying parent, or anorexia – I learned the only way to keep going forward was to conquer each one.

Of course, I haven't done all this drilling, blasting, driving and climbing alone. I've had much help from family, friends, faith, and one rather unique source – figure skating.

Addiction, Job Loss, and Single Parenting

In my twenties, I realized I couldn't take another step forward in my life without giving up drugs, drinking, and a toxic relationship. I would have never made it over that mountain without the support of family and friends – and deep faith that I would be happier on the other side of this destructive lifestyle. Although, sometimes that faith was "borrowed" from others until I believed on my own.

When I lost my job years later, family stepped in. A single mom with a then six-year-old son, I sat in my apartment one day wondering how I was going to buy food when my parents called and invited me to stay with them in Florida. On the other side of that mountain, I found a great job, regrouped, and got back on my feet emotionally and financially.

Facing an Eating Disorder

Eventually, I remarried and my husband and I raised my then 11-year-old son and two more sons. During these years, I faced one of my toughest internal hurdles – an eating disorder that had been unrecognized since I was a child.

While in therapy for depression, a counselor unearthed my lifelong battle with food and suggested I call the Renfrew Center in Philadelphia. I was surprised when the intake counselor said they would like to admit me that day. I had no idea how dangerously thin I was. This was a major mountain to climb; but, at Renfrew, working with therapists and the beautiful women in my group, I gathered the tools and knowledge I would need to overcome my aversion to food.

The most important skill I gained at Renfrew was how to nurture myself. I always nurtured others, but had to learn to think of myself as a child who needed to eat and quiet that inner voice that yelled, "Don't eat, you'll get fat." To this day, whenever I feel hungry, I can override that message and tell myself it's OK to eat.

Skating Serendipity

When I took up the graceful and grueling sport of figure skating (at the age of 40!), I had no idea it would teach me so much about perseverance – and play such an important part in my battle against anorexia.

I began figure skating as an adult because I practically lived in rinks (I had three boys in travel hockey), I had always been a figure skating fan, and besides, skating looked like fun! It was a natural fit. After mastering all the basic group lesson levels, I joined a figure skating club, and began taking private lessons. After passing required tests in front of judges to demonstrate different levels of jumping, spinning, and ice dancing ability, I was eligible to enter local and regional competitions.

I did well at that level, and my coach encouraged me to enter the first U.S. Figure Skating Adult National Figure Skating Championships in Delaware. To my surprise, I earned a bronze medal! I went on to compete in seven national championships and the first adult international competition in France, earning a nice collection of bronze and silver medals – and one gold medal! Last year, at the age of 61, I competed in ice dancing at nationals for the first time with my new dance partner.

An unexpected byproduct of figure skating was positive body awareness and motivation not to starve myself. To have strong muscles and energy to skate well, I have to eat well. Even now, I veto the urge to skip meals so I am able to skate one to two hours a day, four to five days a week. It is sheer joy. When I'm flying across the ice, jumping, spinning, and dancing, I am totally in the moment and mountains don't exist. It has taught me that anything is possible with hard work and never giving up.

Switching Careers

A few years after my husband's company moved him to another state (I stayed behind in New Jersey to keep the boys in their schools), the marriage weakened and we divorced. My oldest son was in college, but the younger two needed my full attention. I was working in sales, but traveling was incompatible with family needs. Changing careers was a scary mountain to climb because it meant taking steps fulfill a lifelong dream – being a writer.

I began as a freelance reporter at a local weekly newspaper and built on that success as a news and features writer for a larger daily paper. I also began writing for Skating magazine, the official publication of U.S. Figure Skating, which gave me incredible opportunities to cover figure skating events and interview such stars as Michelle Kwan, Peggy Fleming, Dorothy Hamill, Brian Boitano, and other elite athletes. Finally, I was a nationally published writer! Still climbing, I accepted a full-time reporter and editor position at a central New Jersey newspaper, where I went on to become editor of a magazine.

When a Parent Needs You

Doesn't it seem that, as soon as you conquer one mountain, another one is around the corner? While working at the newspaper and magazine, my father died, and a year later, my mother's diagnosis of terminal cancer required a major decision. Without hesitation, I left my job, my home, and friends and moved back to New York to help my brothers care for her.

Although this was the saddest time of my life – I still miss my mom so much – it was a blessing to be a part of her life in such an intimate and important way and help make her last days easier. Like many hurdles, however, there are often surprising blessings on the other side. Because of my move, I found the job of a lifetime – a full-time position as a corporate writer and editor. Thanks to a mountain conquered, I had met my goal of being a professional and well-paid writer.

Yes, along came the next mountain! In a struggling economy, it was no surprise when the company where I worked downsized and eliminated my position (along with many co-workers) when the state cancelled contracts. Faced with a major life choice in my sixties, and retirement in sight, I talked with my sons and good friends about my options. I decided to bore a hole through this mountain by going back to college. A few credits short of my bachelor's degree (a goal never realized due to corporate moves or family obligations), this decision will not only fulfill a dream, it will move me closer to reaching my "golden years" goal of working as a freelance writer and editor when I retire. It feels good to be a full-time student again, laying the groundwork for the next part of life's journey.

Lupus

My most recent obstacle almost made me put down my pick axe and blasting caps. A diagnosis of Lupus two years ago explained the episodes of exhaustion, pain, and random loss of motor skills, but raised questions about my ability to keep moving forward. After much prayer, talking with friends and family, and relying on faith, I decided not to let Lupus "flares," stop me from making plans and creating opportunities for work, school, and skating. I asked myself, "What's the worst that could happen"? Maybe I would have to accept a few less freelance jobs, take a few less courses, or cancel a competition, but I could live with that – and I do, every day.

What is life like on the other side?

I never regret or resent any mountain I faced. Each one reinforced my faith and gave me knowledge, tools, and experiences that remind me of life's possibilities, not its limitations. Each one also reinforced my gratefulness for the cadre of friends and family who are always there when I need extra help going through, over or around each obstacle.

On the other side of each mountain, I always found peace and acceptance, and learned to savor each day instead of fretting about the past or worrying about the future. I try to live in the moment and take time to enjoy my family – my brothers, my three sons who are happy and successful, loving, creative and generous people, and two grandchildren who are the light of my life.

No, I'm not an incurable Pollyanna. I'm sure more mountains – as well as those little "bumps" that make the terrain interesting – are waiting down the road. Experience has simply proven, however, that every mountain is worth the dig, the drive, or the climb. It's the only way to get to the other side.

PART 4

7 STEPS TO GETTING ON WITH YOUR LIFE

GET ON WITH YOUR LIFE

Read this statement carefully.

To get what you want out of life,
you must first know what you want out of life.

Sounds obvious, right? Well let me ask you a question: Do you know what you want out of life? I mean, really know what you want.

For many of you, if you are answering the question honestly, you know what you DON'T want.

- You don't want to be poor.
- You don't want to be fat.
- You don't want to be obnoxious.
- You don't want to be [fill in the blank]

That actually is a great start. You read my story. When I was sitting on that curb I knew I did not want to be homeless, carless and penniless.

Discontent with what you don't want can be the fuel that drives you toward what you do want. But you can't stop there. You have got to define what you want out of life. GET ON WITH YOUR LIFE outlines the process for figuring that out.

The process begins with self-knowledge. If you don't know who you are, you will spend your life trying on the masks that others are handing you. You will allow the media and well-meaning friends to tyrannize you with images of what successful people look like, what they do, what they buy and where they live. You will wear yourself out trying to be what others say you should be, rather than becoming the person you were designed to be.

Self-discovery is work. You will need time to think. You will also need a computer or a notebook to write down your thoughts. Resist the temptation to skip over the activities outlined here. Each exercise is designed to help you discover and live your life purpose.

As you get to know YOU and determine what YOU want, you will be able to translate those desires into specific and realistic goals and an action plan for achieving them.

There are also some important 'how-tos' offered in this section.

- How to use your discretionary time effectively,
- How to create an environment of success,
- How to neutralize the emotions that can derail you

These how-tos will help you maintain your progress toward your goals.

As I have said before - Don't worry about perfection. Aim for progress. Each step toward your goals is a step in the right direction. If you need the assistance of a wellness or life coach to keep you on track during the process of change, find one. Consider it an investment in yourself – one of the most important investments you can make.

For additional resources to help you design a life worth living, visit www.lydiamartinez.com.

LIFE STEP ONE:

LEARN FROM THE PAST

Revisiting the past and reflecting on your experiences can provide insight into your fears, your values, your motivations and your inner wisdom. Facing painful memories can help you climb out of the stew of regret, re-wire your thinking and move on.

Adrenaline, the hormone that primes you to run or fight an enemy, also serves to carve memories deeply into your brain. The nature of those memories could be painful or pleasurable; but if adrenaline is released they will stick with you.

That is why daily ordinary repetitive activities are easily forgotten. There is no corresponding adrenaline rush. On the other hand, the heartbreak of getting stilted by your high school boyfriend or girlfriend is something you will remember for the rest of your life.

Remembering bad experiences helps us survive. When the baby touches a hot stove, the adrenaline spikes; the association between stove and pain is forged. Because of this memory, the baby is far less likely to do it again.

Sometimes the associations are not so helpful. Like someone who has survived a car wreck with a red convertible. From that day on, they experience an irrational anxiety whenever they see a red convertible.

Memories etched deep in your brain affect decisions you make today.

They can positively affect you.

Example: You felt joy opening Christmas presents as a kid. That association between Christmas and joy is hard-wired into your brain. Your mood is elevated during the holidays. You enjoy carefully choosing the perfect Christmas gift for each of your loved ones.

They can negatively affect you.

Example: You got lost in a crowd at the state fair as a toddler. The anxiety of losing sight of your mother is hard-wired into your brain. You have totally forgotten the experience, but 'for some unconscious reason' you feel anxiety when you are in crowds.

Revisiting the past and reflecting on your experiences can provide insight into your fears, your values, your motivations and your inner wisdom. Facing painful memories can help you climb out of the stew of regret, re-wire your thinking and move on.

CONSTRUCTING THE LESSONS FROM THE PAST

This exercise will help you shed some baggage that could be impeding your progress toward your goals. It will also help you to understand yourself better so that you can design your life based on what is important to you.

It is a writing exercise. Even just thinking through each question is the first step to GETTING ON WITH YOUR LIFE; but writing it down will anchor the process, and make it more meaningful.

You might not like to 'write' much. That's okay. Just don't totally skip this exercise. Write as little or as much as you want during this exercise. If you need to take a break, do so. Put it down and come back to it later.

- Find a quiet place to sit and reflect.
- Schedule 60 minutes to complete this exercise, but take as long as you want.
- Take out several sheets of paper. At the top of each sheet, write the decades that you have lived so far:

00 – 10 years old [separate sheet]
10 – 20 years old [separate sheet]
20 – 30 years old [separate sheet]
30 – 40 years old [separate sheet]
40 – 50 years old [separate sheet]
50 – 60 years old [separate sheet]

Learn From The Past

GOOD AND BAD MEMORIES

Go through each decade and record the following:

- My strongest painful memories
  [memories that evoke anger, shame, pain, fear, anxiety]

Example: 00 –10: My second grade teacher criticized my penmanship in front of the class. She put one of my papers on the bulletin board with red circles around all the mistakes. My classmates picked on me. I was embarrassed.

- My strongest pleasurable memories
  [memories that evoke pride, happiness, security]

Example: 10-20: I was the first person in my family to graduate from college. It felt good to have my picture taken wearing my graduation gown. My parents were proud of me.

LESSONS LEARNED

Now write down the lesson you learned in each decade from both your positive and your negative experiences. It could be something like this.

Example: 00-10: I learned that saying cruel things to people hurts. I want my words to build people up rather than tear them down.

10-20: I learned that working hard to achieve something feels great.

SKILLS ACQUIRED

List the skills, talents and abilities that you cultivated during each decade. This does not include just formal education, but skills you acquired that you were proud of at the time. This is your resume' of abilities. You are more talented than you think.

Example:

00 – 10: In 5th grade I was asked to write a story. The teacher loved it and gave me an A. She asked me to read it to the class. I learned for the first time that I had the ability to tell a great story.

10 - 20: I learned to drive a car. I got my high school diploma. I was accepted at the college of my choice.

Memories etched deep in your brain affect decisions you make today.

20– 30: I started my own business. I mastered an advanced yoga stretching routine.

ACKNOWLEDGE YOUR ROLE MODELS

Write down the names of people who had a positive influence on your life. Identify what you learned from them.

Example:

Aunt Mary taught me how to drive. Mom and dad were too busy with 5 kids and full time jobs, so she took the time to help me learn. Not only did I learn to drive, but I learned the importance of mentoring others.

My sister stayed with me and kept me entertained during my hospital stay after my bike accident. She taught me the importance of standing by your family in their time of need.

Read through this list and gratefully acknowledge these people. If they are still in your life, give them a call or send them an email letting them know you are grateful for their positive influence in your life.

FORGIVE YOUR OFFENDERS

Write down the names of people who had a powerful negative influence on your life. [Hint: some people might be on both lists.] Focus on the ones that come to mind fairly easily. These are very likely the ones you have yet to forgive.

Example:

Joe – my old boyfriend who rejected me
Christy – a work mate who lied about me to the boss, and got me fired.

- Go through this list and express forgiveness. It will reinforce your commitment to forgive if you speak it out loud.

  Example:

  I forgive you, Joe, for the insensitive way you broke up with me.

- Now shred the list and throw it away.

This does not mean you are excusing the offenders' insensitivity or abuse. It means that you are not going to mentally rake the offender over the coals, in accusation till the day you die. It means you are not going to wallow in fear and walk in distrust of others, just because this person hurt you.

When you refuse to forgive, it doesn't hurt the offender, it hurts you. I heard it said, "It's like drinking poison and waiting for the other person to die."

If you have strong emotions associated with a particular individual you are likely to experience a flare up of emotion again. You can diminish the strength of those memories by consciously relaxing when the emotions rise. The stress hormones strengthen memories. The relaxation hormones - acetylcholine specifically - softens them.

CAVEAT: I am not talking about offenses that are criminal in nature or causing you to act in ways that endanger you. There are times to share information about your experience with the proper authorities so that you are not put at risk. There are times to get professional counseling.

FORGIVE YOURSELF

The only person present in every single one of your memories is YOU. Very likely, there are attitudes you embraced, decisions you made, and words you said that you regret. As these come to mind, write them down. Admit them and say out loud, "I forgive myself for [fill in the blank.]"

Admitting your mistakes is part of the healing process. Denying them is like sweeping dirt under the carpet. It is still there. If you don't come clean, it will manifest as shame in your life.

- Shame will cause you to put on a mask, because if they only knew how you really are they would reject you. So to prevent rejection, something we all fear, we wear a mask instead.

- Shame will cause you to sabotage your success in relationships in business and in life. After all, you don't deserve to succeed.

As you bring your 'screw ups' to light, you get released from the undercurrent of shame and guilt that causes you to sabotage relationships and sabotage your success journey.

Don't forget to cut yourself some slack. Childhood wounds and surrounding circumstances can make you more vulnerable to doing things you regret. Forgive yourself and move on.

If you feel you need to take some action to make things right, do it. You might have to go and ask forgiveness. If you have defrauded someone, you might have to do some restitution. Do what you have to do to make things right - but do FORGIVE YOURSELF.

<u>MOVE ON</u>

Now it is time, to take the lessons you have learned from the past to construct the life you want in the future.

LIFE STEP TWO:

DESIGN YOUR FUTURE

Clarifying what you want takes mental muscle and
emotional sweat. Most of us don't like to think that hard.
But consider the alternative: You either design your future,
or it will be designed for you by your boss, your moods or
the crisis of the day.

If you don't know where you are going, you will probably end up somewhere else. ~ Lawrence J. Peter

Designing your life is simply - 'the process of deciding what you want'. If you know what you want, you can focus your efforts and leverage resources to get what you want.

Clarifying what you want takes mental muscle and emotional sweat. Most of us don't like to think that hard. But consider the alternative: You either design your future, or it will be designed for you by your boss, your moods or the crisis of the day.

Taking time to think through what you want will keep you from floundering through life and ending it with regret. The following exercise will help you:

- **Define your core values.**

  Core values serve as a moral compass to preserve your character and integrity as you pursue your goals.

- **Define your passion.**

  Your passion will fuel your commitment to reach your goals.

- **Develop a 'Do before I Die' list.**

  This is the list of things you wish to accomplish in life. The items on this list must align with both your core values and your passion.

- **Define your life purpose.**

  This is a word picture of what reaching your goals 'looks like' and 'feels like'. Creating the 'emotion of fulfillment' will keep you from being sabotaged by fleeting moods and momentary distractions while in pursuit of your goals.

Grab a paper and pen [or computer, if you prefer]. You will be reflecting on life and writing down your thoughts.

- Don't worry about being eloquent.
- Don't worry about answering the questions perfectly.
- Just complete these exercises to the best of your ability.

STEP ONE: Define your core values

Your values come from a variety of sources: your parents, your faith community, your peer group. As children, for better or worse, we generally embrace the values of our parents [or whatever significant family grouping we are in].

As we venture out into the world, we meet people from other backgrounds. The values we have inherited from our family will be challenged. We will begin to revise our personal values based on our exposure to other ideas.

Some values are superficial. They change based on the stage of life we are in. Example: Being popular in high school.

Design Your Future

Core values are those values that do not change with time. They are the lighthouse of the soul. They offer that clear voice of warning when you are in danger of shipwreck. They offer reinforcement when you are on the right path.

Taking inventory of your life in the previous section equipped you with some insight into the values you are attracted to, as well as values that you recoil from. Bring those insights to this next exercise.

CORE VALUE EXERCISE

- Brainstorm as many phrases and words as you can think of that reflect what is important to you. Tell it like it is.
- List some people you most respect. What qualities do you most admire about them?
- List some people you do not respect. Why do you lack respect for them?
- Finish thiese sentences: I feel really great about myself when I [fill in the blank]

Do you see any patterns? If you find yourself choosing a lot of phrases that fit into the same category, that is an indication of a core value driving your choices.

Example:

Your core value might be being a great parent if:

- *Several phrases pertain to your children [spending time with my kids, being president of the PTA, reading biographies of successful people to my kids].*
- *The people you admire were really great parents, involved in school time activities.*
- *The people you disrespect are those who sacrificed relationships with their kids for a career.*

If being a great parent is a core value - you will have great regrets if you fail at this.

STEP TWO: Find your Passion

You also need to identify the things that launch you out of bed, excited about facing the day.

FIND YOUR PASSION EXERCISE

- List the activities that make you lose track of time.
- List the things that you are naturally good at.
- List the things people typically ask you for help with.
- If you had to teach something, what would you choose to teach?

With those core values and passions in mind, create your 'DO BEFORE I DIE!" list.

STEP THREE: Create your 'Do Before I Die!' list

I hate to be morbid, but we need to face this fact. Life is short. As you wrote out your memories for each decade, it probably dawned on you how quickly life passes. If there are things you want to do before you die, you better figure that out now. That is what the 'Do before I Die' list is all about.

Don't just make a mental list. Research has shown that when you write goals down you are far more likely to accomplish them. Writing your list is like making a contract with yourself.

'DO BEFORE I DIE' EXERCISE

At the end of your life, what will you regret:

- not doing?
- not having?
- not being?

This list can contain the mundane [quit smoking] or the aspirational [launch a non-profit support group for the parents of children with cancer]. It can require time [hike the Appalachian Trail] or money [build a vacation home in the Florida Keys].

Make this list as long as you like.

STEP FOUR: Do a reality check

Answer these 5 questions about EACH item on your list.

- *Do I believe that achieving this is possible?*
- *Do I have a strong desire to achieve this?*
- *Is the timing right for me to commit to achieving this?*
- *Am I willing to invest in the training/education/tools I need to accomplish this?*
- *Am I willing to create and commit to an action plan to achieve this?*

If you cannot answer a resounding 'YES' to each of these questions for a particular item take it off the list.

> **Designing your life is simply - 'the process of deciding what you want'. If you know what you want, you can focus your efforts and leverage resources to get what you want.**

STEP FIVE: What does it look like to achieve your goals

A life purpose statement is a snapshot of what it feels like and what it looks like to have fulfilled your 'Do before I Die' list. You can create a snap shot for whatever time frame you choose.

This life purpose statement will help you emotionalize your goals. It will also stoke your commitment to stay on track in achieving them. Write it in the present tense, as though you are experiencing it now.

- **1 year down the road**

  I have lost 20 lbs. It feels great to get rid of the fat clothes and even better to buy the 'new body' clothes. I really love the ocean front lot Greg and I have chosen for our dream home. What a blessing to have enough money for the down payment.

- **5 years down the road**

  Greg and I have started building our new home. My favorite part is the huge bay window looking out on the beach. I am now down to a size 6 with a tone body. It is wonderful having friends tell me that I look younger than I did 5 years ago. What a blast doing the zip line through the Costa Rican jungle this year. What a joy to find out we are going to have a child. God has truly blessed us.

- **10 years down the road**

  Sitting on the front porch of my beautiful home, listening to the waves hit the ocean shore is truly satisfying. I love hosting parties for friends here. Our child is now in school. It has been great identifying her giftings and having the resources to cultivate them. Our family vacations have been a blast: hiking in the Alps, taking art lessons in Tuscany, camping in Yellowstone, bicycling the Blue Ridge. It is really great to have more than enough to give as well. Over the past 10 years, we have tripled our giving to medical missions throughout the world.

STEP SIX: What does it look like to not achieve your goals

Sometimes nightmares are more powerful than dreams. Imagine what your life will be like if you don't take action to achieve your goals.

- ### 1 year down the road:

  I still feel frumpy and totally cannot stand my job. If I have to share this cubicle with Ernie one more year I think my head will pop off.

- ### 5 Years down the road:

  Rent is merely paying someone else's mortgage. I really want to own a house. I wish I had taken advantage of all the real estate deals 3 years ago. My biological clock is ticking – but there is no way we can afford to have a child.

- ### 10 Years down the road:

  Well my years of eating junk food in front of the TV has caught up with. I just got the news that I am officially type 2 diabetic, just like my mom. I am so done with my job and now they are talking about reducing our benefits. That is exactly why I stayed with this job to begin with! Rent is going up, and it looks like I will never own a home. My health care costs are rising and my health care benefits are shrinking. I am in a black hole of despair.

STEP SEVEN: Start now, start slow, but do start

A journey of a thousand miles begins with one step.
- Chinese proverb

I know that for some of you, just getting through the day is overwhelming, let alone thinking through a lifetime. You are going to have to resist the temptation to 'put off thinking about the future, 'til life is less crazy.'

There will always be a convenient excuse 'for not doing what needs to be done.' It has been said, "Excuses are the tools with which those with no purpose in view build for themselves great monuments of nothing."

If you are overwhelmed, keep it simple. Take one item on your 'DO BEFORE I DIE LIST'. In the next section you will learn how to create a goal statement and action plan to help you achieve that item.

I assure you, if you take one small step in the direction of your dreams, that one small step will energize you to take the next step and the next and the next and the next.

Here is a beautiful, real life example of a 'Life Purpose Statement'. Michelle does an excellent job, 'taking a snapshot' of the future. She is very articulate. You don't have to be this eloquent, but do your best to envision what you want.

Life Purpose Statement by Michelle Hepfler

It is August 2017 and we are living in Cambria, California. We reside in a 5 bedroom, 3 1/2 bath home that sits on 140 acres. It is surrounded by herbal, floral, and vegetable gardens that are well maintained by the gardener. I can see the oceans and the mountains .... The scenery is breathtaking and looks like a postcard.

The 6 dogs and 5 horses keep me in shape, along with a personal trainer that comes to the house 3 times per week. The academic training center accommodates 100 people for business and Family Spirituality seminars. Oh look, Eve and Don are returning from a morning horseback ride …those 2 are inseparable.

Our life here is everything we have hoped for. Achieving 2 residual incomes exceeding $300,000 through my direct sales business and $100,000 through Real Estate investments in March 2013, made this all come true. Spending the last year in Australia was a growing experience for our family and our business.

I have been blessed with 3 beautiful, articulate, and intelligent children who love God with their whole heart. I am so proud of each one of them and their individual talents. Don is a loving, compassionate and patient husband and father. I adore and respect him unconditionally. I am so proud of the man he has become. He continues to grow in his faith through spearheading family workshops in our training facility. His CD's and books have gained national recognition and are found in Christian book stores across the country. I am active in the church choir and Don continues to lector. The children love the Sunday programs.

I have just returned from a book signing tour, I Put My Make Up On With An Elmo Mirror - a tips book for new moms. Presently, I am working on my second book, Behind The Chair, More Than You Really Wanted To Know, a salon coffee table book. I know it will be an instant success.

I continue to grow my direct sales business. This opportunity has blessed and enriched my life that words cannot describe … the people … the people. It truly is about the people and helping others. I continue to be a magnet for positive, goal oriented people who are looking for an opportunity, a vehicle to allow them the life they deserve.

My greatest achievement thus far is The Rosemary Jane Center, a foster home for 25 children, ages 0-18. The facility is warm, spiritual, and beautiful with expansion plans on the horizon. The staff has the hearts of angels and the patience of saints. The retailing of my CD's created the income necessary for this foundation.

Family visits are routine. I fly immediate family out on a regular basis to enjoy the countryside and best of all, to enjoy the children. Family is the most important and the time and love we share creates the memories that mold us.

I love the life Don and I have created. I am blessed with family, health, and wealth – But the greatest gift and blessing is God's unconditional love. This love allows me the spiritual roots to grow personally and professionally and to care for myself and my family. Thank You God, for what you have given me.

LIFE STEP THREE:

SET GOALS, DETERMINE ACTIONS

The more emotionally attached you are to your goal
– the more determined you will be in reaching it.
The more determined you are to reach it
– the more likely you are to succeed.
When you succeed with one goal
– you will begin to create larger goals.
In other words, your dreams will grow as you do.

Each one of you reading this book has a different vision for your life. My intention is to equip you with the skills necessary to fulfill that vision. To fulfill that vision you are going to have to learn how to:

- CLARIFY WHAT YOU WANT [Goal Statement]
- CLARIFY THE STEPS TO GET IT [Action Plan]

Goal setting and action plan development will help you in all areas of life: losing weight, achieving an academic career, starting a business or whatever.

Like any skill, you will get better with practice. It's like learning to drive a car. You have to learn the basics first. Once you learn the basics you can take that car wherever you want to go. On the other hand, without the basic skills you won't be leaving the driveway.

GOAL STATEMENT BASICS

- ### A goal must be specific.

I take issue with the 'sacred cow' statement, "Reach for the moon, at least you will land among the stars." This does not make sense on many levels.

What if we planned our trips to visit Grandma's for Thanksgiving dinner with the attitude, "My goal is to get to grandma's. If I head in that direction, at the very least, I will make it to the local diner."

No, you aim for Grandmas and map out the path to get there. True, there might be some unforeseeable and even insurmountable obstacles to getting there – a category 5 hurricane or something – but bar those kinds of things, you will get to Grandma's.

- ### A goal must be emotionally charged.

To stay committed to your goal, it has to be something that arouses a strong emotion. When you read it, you should feel passion - "I must achieve this goal and I will not settle for less!!!!!"

If your goal does not evoke a powerful emotion, you are in danger of never taking action. If you do take action, you are in danger of getting off track.

- **Choose one goal that you would like to accomplish in the next 12 months.**

FOR EXAMPLE: I want to increase my income from $45,000 a year to $90,000 a year within the next 12 months.

- **Now ask yourself – "Am I serious or just kidding around?"**

  Hmmmm.

  – *Would I be satisfied with $85,000?*
    If so pare it down further.

  – *Would I be satisfied with $80,000?*
    If so pare it down further.

  – *Would I be satisfied with $75,000?*
    If so pare it down further.

  – *Keep going until you get to that 'I WILL NOT SETTLE*
    FOR LESS' moment.

I Will Not Settle For Less

'I will not settle for less' then $57,000 a year and I must make it within the next 12 months. You have just whittled your goal down to something specific that arouses your emotions.

Not that I don't believe in dreaming big. I do. But it works like this:

- The more emotionally attached you are to your goal
  - the more determined you will be in reaching it.
- The more determined you are to reach it
  – the more likely you are to succeed.
- When you succeed with one goal
  - you will begin to create larger goals.

In other words, your dreams will grow as you do.

A goal must be purpose-driven.

Ask yourself, "Why?" The more clear you are on this, the more committed you will be to achieving it.

Why do I need to earn $57,000 this year?

BECAUSE I currently earn $45,000 a year but I carry $12,000 in debt. I feel like I will never get ahead. I need to make at least $57,000 to get out from under this debt. So I have to find a way to increase my income by at least $12,000 a year.

A goal must be realistic.

Filter it through the 5 question reality check.

- *Do I believe that achieving this is possible?*
- *Do I have a strong desire to achieve this?*
- *Is the timing right for me to commit to achieving this?*
- *Am I willing to invest in the training/education/tools I need to accomplish this?*
- *Am I willing to create and commit to an action plan to achieve this?*

Does it pass the reality check? If so, you are on your way.

CONGRATULATIONS. You have just created a specific, emotionally charged, realistic and purpose-driven goal. At this point, the pain of NOT reaching your goal exceeds the pain of reaching it. Your likelihood of success has increased dramatically.

A goal must be written.

Your goals are like a promise you make to yourself. When you write them down, you deepen the impression they make on your memory.

Post your written goals where you can read them during the day. This will help you prioritize how you use your time. It will also increase your awareness of the resources available to you to make your goals a reality.

GOAL STATEMENT:

I will not settle for less than an increase of $12,000 in income by December 31st, 2013. This money will be applied to and completely eliminate my credit card debt without lowering my current standard of living.

> *IN SUMMARY:*
>
> A goal must be:
>
> - Specific
> - Emotionally charged
> - Purpose-driven
> - Realistic
> - Written [and read].

ACTION PLAN BASICS

Identify the options for reaching your goal

You are emotionally committed to increasing your income by $12,000 to eliminate your credit card debt. How do you plan to increase your income? List your options:

- *Get a second job? I would need to work 17 hours a week at the going rate of $15 an hour.*
- *Start an after-hours office cleaning service? I would need to secure 5 customers a week, who pay the going rate of $65 per office.*

> **To stay committed to your goal, it has to be something that arouses a strong emotion. When you read it, you should feel passion - "I must achieve this goal and I will not settle for less!!!!!"**

You could actually have a combination of strategies, but for the sake of illustration let's choose one:

I am going to start an after-hours office cleaning service.

Filter it through the 5 question reality check.

- *Do I believe that achieving this is possible?*
- *Do I have a strong desire to achieve this?*
- *Is the timing right for me to commit to achieving this?*
- *Am I willing to invest in the training/education/tools I need to accomplish this?*
- *Am I willing to create and commit to an action plan to achieve this?*

If it makes it through the filter, you are even closer to achieving your ultimate goal of getting debt free by the end of the year.

Identify the obstacles you will need to overcome to achieve your goals

The obstacles that need to be overcome, and how you plan to overcome will become your action plan.

OBSTACLE: Raise the money for supplies [$1500 for the year]

Vacuum Cleaner - $500
Clothes and Brushes - $200/year
Cleaning solutions - $200/year
Business Cards, Letterhead, Stamps - $200
Phone Service – [no additional expense as I need phone anyway]
Gas to and from Job - $25 a month - $300

CAPITAL NEEDED: $1,500

ACTION PLAN:

- *Ask Uncle Ned for a $500 loan. He offered to help me with the expense of starting a small business.*
- *Apply for a small business grant from the County Economic Development Commission. Grants of $1,000 are being offered to business startups in the county. As long as the business idea is sound the county will provide the grant.*

OBSTACLE: Secure 5 clients who pay $65 a week for my cleaning services.

ACTION PLAN FOR SECURING CLIENTS:

Monthly:
Post 40 flyers
Make 20 sales calls

That means each week:
I post 10 flyers
I make 5 sales calls

That means each day:
I post 2 flyers
I make 1 sales call

Monitor and adjust your progress

Ask yourself at the end of the week:

- *Did I take the actions that I said I would take?*

  If not you have to decide:

  - Do I adjust my action plan to fit into my life?
  - Do I adjust my life to fit into my action plan?

- *Did it produce the results I expected it to?*

  If not you have to decide:

  - Do I need to increase the # of flyers and calls?
  - Do I need to better qualify the places I am putting flyers?
  - Do I need to make more sales calls?

Add your action plan to your goal statement

GOAL STATEMENT

I will not settle for less than an increase of $12,000 in income by December 31st, 2013. This money will be applied to and completely eliminate my debt, without lowering my current standard of living.

I will raise the money through starting an office cleaning business.

To capitalize my business I will secure a loan from Uncle Ned and a grant from the County Small Business commission.

I will Secure 5 weekly clients who are willing to pay $65 each week for cleaning service. I estimate it will take me 2 hours per office each week.

I will apply $1,000 a month to my credit card debt. The balance will be applied to cover my loans and overhead.

Add a statement that envisions the payoff

It is December 2013. It feels wonderful to have earned enough money to get debt-free. I sleep better. I am happier. I can now begin to apply that $1,000 a month to other things. I want to buy a new car. I want a 2014 VW Passat and new furniture. My reputation is growing. I now need to hire some assistants to handle the extra work.

IN SUMMARY:

These are the steps to constructing your action plan.

1. Identify the options for reaching your goal.
2. Identify the obstacles you will need to overcome to achieve your goals. Your action plan consists of the steps you need to overcome these obstacles.
3. Monitor and adjust your progress.
4. Add your action plan to your goal statement.
5. Add a statement that envisions the payoff.

There is something powerful about setting a firm goal. Your determination to reach your goal has a magnetic effect. It's known as the Law of Attraction. Some interpret that law to mean - if you declare what you want, what you need to achieve what you want will be magically provided.

I see it differently. As you commit to a goal you will become aware of and attracted to the resources you need to achieve that goal. Success does not result from sitting around, dreaming big and waiting for opportunities to come to you. Success will come when you figure out what you want - when you figure out what you need to do to get what you want - and when you roll up your sleeves and do it.

LIFE STEP FOUR:

USE YOUR TIME PURPOSEFULLY

Is it hitting home for you? Time has boundaries!
Even for mega-achievers like Martha Stewart or the
President of the United States. You cannot do it all.
That is why it is important to be very clear on what you
want out of life. How you use your time will determine
whether you live a satisfying life or one filled with regret.

Time is free, but it's priceless. You can't own it, but you can use it. You can't keep it, but you can spend it. Once you've lost it you can never get it back. Harvey Mackay

Each day we are given a fresh batch of time - a whole 24 hours of it. No more, no less. Some of those hours are spoken for, but all of us have time that we can use as we choose. It's called discretionary time.

Identifying how much discretionary time you have can help you to make important decisions on how to use it. The discretionary time available to each of us varies. For the sake of illustration, let's look at a fairly typical day, for the person who has a standard job.

- **SLEEP [8 hours]:** Most of us need around 8 hours of sound shut-eye each night.

- **JOB/COMMUTE [11 hours]:** 1 hour getting ready [showering, dressing, eating a healthy breakfast and the morning cup of Joe], 8 hours working, 30 minutes for lunch, 90 minutes to commute.

- **ERRANDS/CHORES/MEALS [2 hours]:** This includes the other routine activities, errands and chores.

- **TIME LEFT AT THE END OF THE DAY [3 hours]** This 3 hours left over after you do whatever needs to be done is your discretionary time.

- **WEEKENDS [16 hours]:** After sleep and errands let's say you have 8 hours of discretionary time on Saturday and Sunday. [You might have more. You might have less].

TOTAL DISCRETIONARY TIME: 31 hours a week

Is it hitting home for you? Time has boundaries! Even for mega-achievers like Martha Stewart or the President of the United States. You cannot do it all.

That is why it is important to be very clear on what you want out of life. How you use your time will determine whether you live a satisfying life or one filled with regret.

The best use of your discretionary hours is to use them doing things that are important to you. Spend your time doing things that are consistent with your core values, your passion and your life purpose.

To determine whether you are investing your discretionary time wisely or not, you have to make some observations and do some calculations.

QUESTION: What are your priorities?

Let's say your priorities are:

- **FAMILY [Top priority]**
- **CHURCH**
- **HEALTH AND FITNESS [Everyone should have this as a priority]**
- **MUSIC**

Think back through this past week.

QUESTION: How much time did you spend serving those priorities?

- **FAMILY** [Top priority]
  Watched daughter play soccer [2 hours]
  Date night with husband [2 hours]

Use Your Time Purposefully

- **CHURCH**
  Sunday Worship [2 hours]
  Bible Study [2 hours]

- **FITNESS**
  Walked Dogs [2 hours]

- **MUSIC**
  Guitar Lesson and practice [3 hours]

TOTAL: 14 hours committed to your priorities.

QUESTION: How were the other 17 hours spent?

- **TELEVISION** – 10 hours
  Nielson [a national TV ratings corporation] reports that the average American watches TV 5 hours a day. I would assume much of that watching is in the background of doing other things. Nonetheless – that is a whopping 35 hours a week. So, let's assume that 10 hours is 'concentrated' watching. I am not against TV, but it is important to see where it lands in your priorities.

- **COMPUTER TIME** – 7 hours
  This would include emails, social media and surfing.

Television or computer time might be a priority for you. I'm not judging you. I am just suggesting you decide whether it is or it isn't a priority. If it is, by all means put it on the calendar.

If you look at this example, you can see that although FAMILY was listed as the top priority, the discretionary time spent with FAMILY was relatively low.

Hmmm. This tells you, if your core values and life purpose has something to do with being a great parent and loving spouse, you will regret using your time to watch TV rather than doing things with the spouse and kids.

By practicing a few simple disciplines, you can use your time more effectively.

Determine how many discretionary hours you have each week.

You have a unique life. Your pool of discretionary hours might be bigger or smaller then this example. Take time to figure how many hours you can call your own.

Determine your priorities.

In this illustration the priorities are FAMILY, CHURCH, FITNESS and MUSIC.
You priorities might be different. For example: you might be starting a business with the goal of creating more time freedom so that you can spend more time with your family. For the next year, BUSINESS-BUILDING might be a priority that is consistent with your FAMILY priority.

You determine what YOUR priorities are.

Brainstorm what you want to accomplish each week

- Write down everything that comes to mind.

Purge that list of anything inconsistent with your priorities

- Put a check mark beside each item that is consistent with your priorities [FAMILY, CHURCH, FITNESS]

- Eliminate everything that does not serve that priority.

Schedule your time consistent with those priorities.

It is important to not only decide what you want to accomplish, but to put those things on your calendar. Writing them on your calendar will prevent you from falling into the time-wasting trap.

Transfer items that don't get done.

The things that you did not accomplish, that you wished
to, can be transferred to the next week. If you find yourself,
never getting around to doing them, you might consider
taking it off your list. It might not be as important as you
think.

*Each day we are given a
fresh batch of time - a whole
24 hours of it. No more, no
less. Some of those hours are
spoken for, but all of us have
time that we can use as we
choose.*

FIND WAYS TO CREATE MORE TIME:

Become efficient.

How about those 60 minutes you use to get ready for work? Could you take a shorter shower
and spend less time in front of the mirror, so you have an extra 15 minutes to walk the dog in
the morning. [FITNESS]

How about household chores? Ask yourself, does the house really need to be deep cleaned
each week? Can you afford to hire someone to do it for you?

Life's projects are endless. Figure out what is important to get done. Do that and forget the rest.

Declutter your environment.

Clutter wastes a lot of your time. One study estimated we spend up to an hour a day looking for
things. That is 7 hours a week! If you are covered up with clutter, take time to dig yourself out.

Simplify your commitments.

Sometimes you have to sacrifice the good, for the best. Seriously think through all your commitments. Any that are not consistent with your priorities, eliminate.

Manage communication.

We are perpetually connected - email, cell phones, Twitter and other social media. It is easy to
sit down to answer an email that should take minutes and get pulled into the lure of checking
Facebook one more time, or reading that email that you are only mildly interested in. Before
you know it you have squandered hours. If you schedule connection time and stick to your
schedule, it will open up more time for you to focus on what is truly important.

Leverage your time.

As often as possible, do things that fulfill more than one priority. For example:

FAMILY AND FITNESS go together beautifully. Plan a hike at the local National Park with your spouse and kids. Practice soccer with your daughter.

FAMILY, MUSIC AND CHURCH: Learn some hymns on your guitar to play at your weekly bible study. And, but of course, take your family.

Don't forget, you share something in common with all the great achievers in the world. Bill Gates, Leonardo Da Vinci and Mother Theresa and every other human who has ever lived, were given the same number of hours in a day – 24. Use them wisely and you will fulfill your life's purpose. Squander them and you will live a life of regret.

LIFE STEP FIVE:

MAKE A LIVING, HAVE A LIFE

I am going to assume that when you review your 'Do Before
I Die' list, you are beginning to see a pattern.
The pattern is - if I am going to actually do these things
before I die, I need 2 things: time and money.
This means, unless you have been handed a trust fund, or
you are independently wealthy, you will have to find a way
to make a living that offers time freedom as well.

I am going to make an assumption here. I am going to assume that when you review your 'Do Before I Die' list, you are beginning to see a pattern. The pattern is - if I am going to actually do these things before I die, I need 2 things: time and money. This means, unless you have been handed a trust fund, or you are independently wealthy, you will have to find a way to make a living that offers time freedom as well.

Let's look at your options:

- **Work at a low skill job, by the hour.**

  In other words, barely eke out a living. This is not the best way to create either time freedom or money.

- **Work for a salary in a profession or trade.**

  The income potential is higher, but you might not have a lot of independence. You will be on someone else's clock. If you love what you are doing, that might not matter. If time freedom is important make sure you choose a profession that offers flexibility.

- **Start a business.**

  Based on statistics, you have a higher likelihood of increasing your income and controlling your time if you own your own business.

  If you want to start a business, do so carefully. A business isn't something you can choose off the shelf like a pair of shoes. It is not an impulse buy. There are risks. The vast majority of businesses fail within their first 5 years. This means the business that started to make a profit, actually lost money, maybe lots of money.

  To be successful - and profitable - a business should be something that matches your abilities, interests, and skills. You will also need start-up capital and customers for your products or services.

  Here is a short list of some low-risk business options. These businesses require minimal start-up capital and can be operated from your home. There are plenty of other possibilities, but to stimulate your thinking, here are a few.

  - **Website and Management**: There has been a shift in how business is done. Many 'brick and mortar' businesses are closing and creating a less expensive and more easily accessed presence on the internet. Due to this shift, the demand for website-related services is growing. Unless you already have the know-how, you'll need to spend some time learning the technology, but there are opportunities in this field.

- **Graphic Artist**: If you are an artist, you might consider a business where you design logos and other marketing materials.

- **Virtual Assistant**: There are companies that are looking for individuals who can provide temporary services from home. You might do medical or legal transcription or provide information technology services.

- **Freelance writer**: If you have a knack for writing, you can earn money writing for others. Perhaps writing blogs or newsletters.

- **Online Store**: Products can be sold through Ebay [resell items] or Etsy [sell handmade goods] or even your own website.

- **Develop an income producing system**

Make A Living and Have A Life

If you own a business you make money when the 'doors are open' and you are working. If you walk away the income dries up.

With an income producing system you invest money or sweat on the front end to gain a higher return on the back end. A successful system will produce income, even when you are not 'on the clock.'

Some options are:

- **Stocks, Bonds, Commodities** This can be a way to Invest your money and let it earn money for you. There are risks. The value of these investments can up or down. The rule of thumb is - do not invest any more than you can afford to lose. That's the problem. You might not be able to afford to lose anything. Be sure to seek the guidance of a credible financial consultant.

- **Real Estate** There are always opportunities in the real estate market. There are risks, as well. If people aren't buying, you could be holding onto your real estate investment for longer than you like. If the market goes down, you might have to sell at a price lower than you planned. If you are renting your real estate, your income is dependent on the renter's diligence to pay their rent on time. Be sure to seek the guidance of a trustworthy professional who knows the market and its opportunities.

- **Intellectual Property** Books and inventions can produce ongoing royalties. If you have the talent to produce intellectual property and the knowledge to sift through the publishing or patenting process, this is a possibility.

- **Direct selling [AKA Network marketing]** This can be an attractive option for those without much capital to start a business. It can be started with very little money, operated from the home with little overhead. Direct selling has the potential to produce ongoing income through recruiting others who also sell products or services. But there are also many risks. The drop-out rate is high.

  Be sure to do your homework. Find a company that offers the following.

  - **Longevity**: Find a company that has been in business for at least 5 years. Ground floor start-ups can sound enticing, but they are risky.

  - **Training**: A solid company will provide training, not just 'motivational' training, but training on 'how to' build and manage a sales organization and reliable product knowledge training.

  - **Diversity**: In order to remain competitive in the marketplace there needs to be diversity in the product line.

  - **Financial Stability**: Check out the annual reports. Is the company making money? If they don't offer a way for you to investigate the financial status, run.

  - **Regulatory Stability**: Is the company abiding by the rules? What is their status with the Better Business Bureau or the state Attorney General's office? Be sure to find out.

Develop multiple income streams

We often hear about the importance of diversifying investments, but diversifying your income streams is just as important, particularly in difficult economic times. Essentially this means developing multiple income producing sources. There are many ways to configure a menu of income streams. Here is an example of a configuration.

- FULL TIME JOB
- STOCKS – Invest your money, to make more money.
- SIDE BUSINESS – Open a direct-selling distributorship.
- INTELLECTUAL PROPERTY – Write a book, sell on the internet.

However you choose to make a living, be sure to choose something that is a good fit for you. We are all different. One person might love drawing pictures all day long. Another person would be bored to death. One person might love managing a huge project. Another person might be reduced to a blithering idiot if they were put in charge. The wrong match with the wrong income producing activities can make your life miserable.

> *You spend many hours earning a living. Do your homework to ensure that your time is being well spent.*

Knowing who 'YOU ARE" will help you zero in on the business/career you are mostly to succeed at. It will also help you to cultivate strategic alliances with partners who have strengths that you do not have.

Before you choose your living, do a careful self-evaluation. Here are a few questions to stimulate your thinking:

Do you gravitate toward positions of leadership?
YOUR MOTIVATION: Being the best and being in charge.
STRENGTHS: Not easily intimidated, hard worker.
WEAKNESSES: Too forceful and impatient.
POSSIBLE CAREERS/BUSINESS: Ceo, Business-builder.
POSSIBLE STRATEGIC ALLIANCE: Partners who have are strong in the areas on empathy.

Are you attracted to noble causes?
IS YOUR MOTIVATION: To change the world for the better.
STRENGTHS: Ethical and enthusiastic.
WEAKNESSES: Perfectionistic and demanding.
POSSIBLE CAREER/BUSINESS: Start a Non-profit that specializes in your passion.
POSSIBLE STRATEGIC ALLIANCE: Partners strong in public relations.

Do you enjoy making someone happy?
IS YOUR MOTIVATION: To make people happy?
YOUR STRENGTHS: Customer oriented. Loves to advise and assist others.
YOUR WEAKNESSES: Forgets to take care of self.
YOUR POSSIBLE CAREER/BUSINESS: Customer Service, Retail business.
YOUR POSSIBLE STRATEGIC ALLIANCE: Partners with strengths in time-management.

Do you like to research and analyze data?
YOUR MOTIVATION: To systematically solve problems.
YOUR STRENGTHS: Get the facts before taking action.
YOUR WEAKNESSES: Slow to take action.
YOUR POSSIBLE CAREERS/BUSINESS: Engineering, Computer Science.
YOUR POSSIBLE STRATEGIC ALLIANCES: Partners with strong networking and marketing abilities.

Are you highly motivated to 'Get er done'?
YOUR MOTIVATION: To set goals and achieve them.
YOUR STRENGTHS: Optimistic, encouraging and a can-do attitude.
YOUR WEAKNESSES: Impulsive, overcommits, easily bored.
YOUR POSSIBLE CAREERS/BUSINESS: Sales, Motivational Speaking.
YOUR POSSIBLE STRATEGIC ALLIANCES: Partners with accounting and administrative skills.

Are you happiest alone, immersed in a creative project?
YOUR MOTIVATION: To do something creative.
YOUR STRENGTHS: Offers unique abilities and perspectives.
YOUR WEAKNESSES: Sensitive to criticism.
YOUR POSSIBLE CAREERS/BUSINESS: Writer, graphic designer, musician.
YOUR POSSIBLE STRATEGIC ALLIANCES: Partners with business management skills.

Are you motivated to help people in need?
YOUR MOTIVATION: To be an agent of healing.
YOUR STRENGTHS: Calm and thoughtful.
YOUR WEAKNESSES: Tendency to Burn out.
YOUR POSSIBLE CAREER/BUSINESS: Healing professions, counseling.
YOUR POSSIBLE STRATEGIC ALLIANCES: Partners with scheduling and marketing skills.

More than likely you have gifts in more than one area. Look at Bill Gates, the founder and CEO of Microsoft. Bill obviously is gifted in both research and analysis, and getting 'er done. He seems to have found the perfect partner in his wife, Melinda. She is motivated to help people in need. Together they embody a beautiful 2 point strategy: Create wealth, funnel it into meaningful projects.

Bottom line: You spend many hours earning a living. Do your homework to ensure that your time is being well spent. Make sure that what you choose will provide what you want in life: Time, money and satisfaction.

LIFE STEP SIX:

CREATE AN ENVIRONMENT OF SUCCESS

It takes time to remodel your environment - your mind,
your workspace and your relationships. But every positive
change you make, increases the likelihood of fulfilling
your life purpose.

What goes on in our head, in our home, and in our work-place can either support our goals or undermine them. It is important to create an environment of success.
This means you might have to do some remodeling in 5 key areas of your life.

- **Your Physical Space**
  Do your surroundings motivate or frustrate your goals?

- **Your Mind**
  Do your thoughts build you up or tear you down?

- **Your Image**
  Does your presentation of yourself make a good or bad impression?

- **Your Professional Associations**
  Do you network with people who can help you reach your goals?

- **Your Friend Circle**
  Do your friends encourage your commitment to success or resent it?

REMODEL YOUR PHYSICAL SPACE

Envision what a productive day 'looks like'. What are the behaviors that contribute to your success in reaching your goals? Those success behaviors might include:

- Reading your goal statement.
- Going to the kitchen and fixing a low glycemic breakfast.
- Taking a few moments to organize your daily To Do list.
- Picking up the phone and calling that important client.

Ask yourself - How can I create a physical environment that triggers me to do these activities consistently? For example:

- *Is it important to start your day with a healthy breakfast?*

  ENVIRONMENTAL CHANGE: Have those healthy breakfast foods in the cupboards.

- *Is reading your goal statement first thing in the morning important for helping you focus on your priorities?*

- ENVIRONMENTAL CHANGE: Post that goal statement where you can see it first thing in the morning – like on the wall near the toilet [very likely you will be visiting there at some point] or on the bathroom mirror.

- *Is it important to make calls to prospective clients each day?*

  ENVIRONMENTAL CHANGE: Have a contact list prepared and placed near your phone. This will strengthen your commitment to make those calls.

As you go through your day, make a list of things you can change in your physical environment that will help support your goals.

For those of you who are naturally organized, you might, through a few simple tweaks, have your environment organized in a matter of hours. For those of you living in utter chaos, it might require an ongoing long term commitment to create a physical environment of success.

A Successful Environment

The key is this. Take it one step at a time. Perhaps, today the only thing you got done is to post your goal statement where you can see it. That is one small step in the right direction. As you consistently chip away at the chaos, be assured, order will emerge.

Some items you might put on your list:

- Keep healthy food in the kitchen
- Have some convenience foods on hand when you are pinched for time
- Keep an extra water bottle in the frig, ready to grab
- Have your supplements collected in one place within easy reaching distance
- Keep motivational audios in the car.
- Post your goal statements by the frig and the bathroom mirror
- Keep a notebook/calendar [electronic or paper] for recording tasks and appointments.
- Purchase 4 bins:
  - One to collect bills
  - One to collect materials you want to read later
  - One to recycle junk mail as it arrives
  - One for pens, pencils, a stapler, paper clips

Warning!

- Do not become so obsessive about organizing your environment that it sabotages other goal-oriented activities. You do not need the perfect environment to 'get on with your life'.

- Don't use an imperfect environment as an excuse to fail. Everyone has environmental challenges. Some live in small spaces with a growing family. Some can't afford all the state of the art tools yet. Many successful enterprises have been launched from humble environments such as a garage or a kitchen table. Work with what you've got.

REMODEL YOUR MIND

The bible says, "Be transformed by the renewing of your mind." The tools of mind transformation include everything we listen to and read. It works like this.

- What goes into your mind will affect your self-talk.
- Your self-talk will determine how you feel about yourself.
- How you feel about yourself will affect what you do.
- What you do each day will determine your destination.

Mind Renewal Tip #1: Sit at the feet of those who have succeeded

If you are going to succeed, you need to listen to and read things that contribute to the mindset of success. Some mind-enriching activities include:

Read success stories. Take what you learn from the lives of others and apply it to your success journey. With each success story, you will absorb insights and encouragement.

Listen to motivational audios. For very little investment you can purchase or download motivational audios from some of the leading success speakers of all time. Audio books are great. Merely listening, even when they can't have your full attention, will help you absorb on a subconscious level empowering information.

Attend seminars. It is really powerful to be face to face with those whom you respect. It not only enriches your understanding of how to create success in your life, but at events like this you will be networking with like-minded individuals. This will help you cultivate positive friendships.

Mind Renewal Tip # 2: Coach and Encourage Yourself
It's called positive affirmation. To affirm means to say edifying and empowering things to yourself, consistently throughout the day - things that build you up, rather than tear you down.

It means talking to yourself as you would to a much loved child or a close friend. If a 5 year old was learning how to tie her shoes and making a mess along the way, a good mother would not cut her down. No, she would speak encouragement. *'You are getting there. You are on your way to tying your shoes perfectly'.*

The effect of consistent affirmations over time is power-ful. Affirmations re-wire your responses to life. They trigger hormones that cause you to feel serene and focused, rather than rattled and distracted. They can transform your physi-cal posture from shuffling insecurity, to walking tall with a confident swagger.

> *What goes on in our head, in our home, and in our work-place can either support our goals or undermine them.*

There are three categories of affirmation.

- **Responsive Affirmations**: Processing what is going on throughout the day in a positive and helpful way.
- **Proactive Affirmations**: Repetitive reminders that cultivate a positive mindset.
- **Rewards**: The pat on the back you need to keep going.

Let's look at those categories more closely.

- <u>**RESPONSIVE AFFIRMATIONS**</u>: There is an ongoing monologue in your head as you go through your day. Sometimes this mind-chatter is loud. Sometimes it is like 'white noise'; you are oblivious to what you are saying to yourself. Oblivious or not, this monologue will defeat you or empower you.

  - **Listen to yourself**. What do you say to yourself on a daily basis? I will bet that many of you say things to yourself that you would not even consider saying to a close friend. If you did, they would no longer be your friend.

  - **Cancel negative talk and replace it with a positive.** For example: Your exercise goal was to walk briskly each day. You scheduled a block of time to get in your 30 minute brisk walk. For the past two days, you have chosen to surf Facebook during your scheduled 'walking time'. The inner conversation begins.

    NEGATIVE TALK: *Boy, are you a loser! You have been lying to everyone. You are lazy, lard butt. Why even try? You aren't going to walk every day. Why kid yourself?*

    Does this conversation help you feel more confident and empowered? I don't think so. How about this instead?

POSITIVE TALK: *Wow, I missed my walk again. Facebook is a great way to connect but I need to connect after I walk. I still have some day light, I am going to walk for 30 minutes. What a blessing to have control of what I choose to do after work in the evenings. [Reaching for calendar] Starting tomorrow I will schedule social media time as a reward for fulfilling my commitment to walk. Aligning my behavior with my goals is not only possible, it is easy.*

- **PROACTIVE AFFIRMATION** These are the healthy things you say to yourself to set the positive tone in your head. Your goal statement is a type of proactive affirmation. Reading it and speaking it will affirm your commitment to reaching your goals.
You can also develop short descriptive statements reflecting your goals. These affirmations should be memorable, present tense and powerful. Create your own, or borrow others.

  <u>**WEIGHT LOSS AFFIRMATIONS**</u>:
  I burn fat with ease.
  Eating well is a life of abundance and health.

  <u>**SELF ESTEEM AFFIRMATIONS**</u>
  I am confident and enthusiastic about life.
  The talents I have are all I need to live the life I choose to live.

  <u>**SUCCESS AFFIRMATIONS**</u>
  I enjoy doing the things that lead me to my goal.
  Nothing can stop me from working my action plan.

Post them where you can read them. Speak them throughout the day [silently or out loud depending on the circumstance]. This will help you crowd out the negative chatter in your head.

- **REWARDS** We are designed to work for rewards. When we reward ourselves for milestones reached, it creates positive association in our brain. This reinforces our commitment to continuing that behavior.

  Rewards can take many forms, but should ideally be something that's tied to your goal, For example: Let's say your daily goal is to book 3 appointments each day. A reward might be to buy yourself that smart-phone you want. You could have a jar on your desk, and for every time you book an appointment add a dollar to the jar to use toward the phone purchase.

  Or perhaps your goal is to de-clutter your office space and you love flowers. You might reward yourself with a bouquet of fresh flowers for your desk after you have cleaned things up.

REMODEL YOUR IMAGE

You only have one opportunity to make a first impression. Take time to think through the impression you want to make. Not only will presenting yourself well increase the respect others have for you, it will increase your self-respect.

Here are a few basic business courtesies that can enhance the impression you make.

Be punctual. If you arrange to meet someone at a specific time, do whatever you have to do to be there exactly on time. Being late is rude. When you are late, it sends a message that you think your time is more valuable than the other person's.

Stand tall and make eye contact. Your body language is an important element in creating the right first impression. When you meet someone for the first time, stand tall, face the individual square on, and establish eye contact with that person.

Smile and be friendly. This will put the other person at ease and creates a positive impression of you.

Have a firm handshake. Note I said firm, not bone crunching.

Respond politely when you are introduced. Whenever you are introduced to someone, respond by saying either: "How do you do, Mrs. Jones?" or "Nice to meet you, Mrs. Jones." Use the individual's name to make them feel important. It will also help you to remember it.

Remember names: Calling people by their names sends a positive message that you care enough to remember their names.

Do not interrupt people when they are talking. Be patient and let the other person finish what he or she is saying before you respond or attempt to make another point.

Dress appropriately: Women, avoid wearing revealing clothing that shows too much bare skin. Men, don't forget to tuck in your shirt and hike up your pants. Choosing appropriate business attire is an important investment. To simplify your life, choose clothing that is "stain-resistant" and "wrinkle-resistant". Make sure your clothes fit well. Before you walk out the door, look in the mirror. Ask someone for feedback.

Get rid of the gum and toothpicks: Chewing gum or chewing on a toothpick when you are dealing face-to-face with customers or co-workers is unprofessional.

Don't groom yourself in public. No one wants to watch you combing your hair, filing your nails or picking your teeth. Speaking of grooming, be sure to clean your teeth, comb your hair, and wear deodorant.

Cover your mouth when you can't stop a yawn, cough or sneeze. After yawning, coughing or sneezing, say, "Excuse me."

I know that is really basic stuff. But the little things make a big difference. You only have one chance to make a good first impression.

REMODEL YOUR PROFESSIONAL ASSOCIATIONS

It is important to network with two categories of people.

- Like-minded people who are modeling an attitude of success
- Strategic allies that can help you get what you want as you help them get what they want

A good way to do this is to find networking groups. Make an effort to participate in at least two groups that can help you connect to others. There are several types:

- Casual Mixers – Chamber of commerce, Business networks
- Online Media – Facebook, Linked in, e-cademy to name a few.
- Knowledge-based – professional associations with those in a similar profession

Remember, networking is for cultivating rapport, not overwhelming someone with your sales pitch. When you enter networking function, look for individuals standing alone or in a small configuration. Approach and introduce yourself.

Your primary activity should be asking questions and listening to the answers. When you are truly interested in what another has to say, they are more likely to be interested in what you have to say. When you ask questions, they are likely to reciprocate and ask you questions. This gives you an opportunity to share who you are and why you are there.

When it comes to online media, don't be spamming your friends with ads and sales pitches. Use the media to provide a service – entertain, inform and inspire. It is a tool for relationship-building. If you are heavy-handed on the 'Boy, do I have a deal for you' spiels you are at risk of being de-friended.

REMODEL YOUR FRIEND CIRCLE

As you carve out your success path, you will discover who your true friends are. Your true friends will encourage you to be the best that you can be. They will be your cheerleaders. Others will feel threatened by your efforts and passively or even aggressively attempt to sabotage you. It is a tough thing to do, but if you cannot change the people are with, you will need to CHANGE the people you are with.

Obviously, there are people that you cannot entirely cut off: parents, children or spouses. Though you might still have to spend time with them, it is important to minimize the effect they have on you. You are not doing them or yourself a favor by allowing their negativity to drain your energy and distract your focus.

Changing the dynamic of your relationship might require an official pronouncement. You might have to communicate your commitment to your goals. Let them know that if they are discouraging you from reaching your goals, through word or deed, you will need to reduce your time together.

Spend time with your true friends. These are the ones who are in your court and cheering you on as you roll toward your goals. True friends will understand that you might need to spend less time together, so you can focus on the activities leading to your goal.

Sometimes where you meet your friends might need to change as well. If the 'hang outs' undermine your commitments, then choose other 'hang outs.' For example, if you are trying to quit drinking, because it interferes with your life purpose, you might need to avoid Thursday night Happy Hour. If you are trying to lose weight, the weekly gorge-fest at the local 'all you can eat' restaurant, might have to go.

It takes time to remodel your environment – your mind, your workspace and your relationships. But every positive change you make increases the likelihood of fulfilling your life purpose.

LIFE STEP SEVEN:

BEWARE OF SELF-SABOTAGE

When you begin to grow personally, this can make family and old friends uncomfortable. Your success, your healthy attitude will make insecure people feel more insecure. In an act of self- preservation they will try to "take you down a notch or two".

Wow! What a journey. By now the fog should be lifting and you should be seeing a glimpse of the life that you want on the horizon. That is the purpose of this no-nonsense guide. My intent is to help you identify your life purpose and move toward it, one step at a time. Every step toward your goals is a step in the right direction.

But I have a concern. I am concerned that you will:

- Read this guide and agree with what is said, but something inside of you keeps you from taking action.

OR

- You will start taking action, begin to experience success and for some reason, it feels foreign and uncomfortable; so uncomfortable that you are tempted to revert to your old life of mediocrity and subsistence living.

It's called self-sabotage. This danger is faced by everyone who has ever tried to break out of the mold others have put them in.

The good news is, self-sabotage is a thought process. It begins in the mind and can be overcome in the mind. Let's talk about those self-sabotaging thoughts.

Self-sabotaging thought: WHO DO YOU THINK YOU ARE?

If you have grown up in an environment controlled by unhealthy authority figures [parents, peers, teachers, bosses] you are in danger of embracing the unhealthy expectations of those unhealthy 'significant others'.

When you attempt to live outside of those expectations you will begin to have an uncomfortable feeling. Psychologists term this feeling as 'cognitive dissonance'. It is defined as an uncomfortable feeling caused by holding two contradictory ideas simultaneously. That uncomfortable feeling is a type of pain.

As humans we are wired to retreat from pain. This is the mechanism that drives addiction. Living life is painful. The 'drug of choice' relieves that pain. Intoxication feels 'familiar and comfortable'. Living in the bold light of reality does not. So to stop the pain, the addict is tempted to retreat back into that old life of addiction.

Hear me - if you strive for personal growth, and achievement, there will be growing pains. Count on it. Your emotional state will have to mature to accommodate the growth and that takes time.

Not only will you have to live through that uncomfortable feeling on the 'inside', your pain will often be compounded by the voices coming at you from the outside.

When you begin to grow personally, this can make family and old friends uncomfortable. Your success, your healthy attitude will make insecure people feel more insecure. In an act of self-preservation they will try to "take you down a notch or two". These friends [aka frenemies] will criticize you, reject you or even gossip about you. If you have not formed new alliances with people who reinforce your success, you are in danger of self-sabotage.

Self-Sabotage

At this point you will be tempted.

- You will be tempted to give up your personal growth.
- You will be tempted to re-align your behavior with those unhealthy expectations.
- You will be tempted to surround yourself with others who also are confined by that unhealthiness.
- You will be tempted to retreat back into the old way of doing things.

Don't!

Self-sabotaging thought: IF PEOPLE REALLY KNEW WHAT I LOSER I AM

This is a common phenomenon that afflicts successful people. Even those who have worked darn hard to get where they often feel like imposters when they become successful. It is actually called the 'imposter syndrome'.

The symptoms include:

- The sense of having fooled other people into overestimating your ability.
- Attributing your success to some factor other than your ability [I was just lucky. I just happened to be in the right place at the right time].
- The fear of being exposed as a fraud.

Self-sabotaging thought: IF YOU DON'T SWEAT, YOU HAVEN'T WORKED

If you were raised in a working class family that prized manual labor 8 hours a day, 5 days a week, you might start to feel a dissonance with work that does not involve physical sweat.

When you begin to leverage your time so that you can make more money in fewer hours using your brain, rather than your brawn, you will feel like this is not real work. It will feel like you are doing something to be ashamed of.

Self-sabotaging thought: MONEY MANAGEMENT IS BAD

You might have come from a family that prized impulsive purchases though they could not really afford them. Instead of acknowledging the unhealthy spending and its effect on their finances they ennobled it. *['Out of control spending is not frivolous', it is generous or even spiritual I don't worry about tomorrow. I live for today.]* When you begin to manage your money, you feel stingy and unspiritual.

Self-sabotaging thought: AWWW SHUCKS!

Perhaps you have been raised in an environment where dismissing your strengths is considered an asset. You might have learned 'false humility'. You feel uncomfortable accepting praise for a job well done or speaking positive affirmations to yourself.

If someone compliments you, you have to bite your tongue to resist the temptation to say, "No really, it was nothing. I really am incompetent and what I do sucks." You find it hard to acknowledge the compliment with a calm and gracious, "Thank you."

Self-sabotaging thought: MONEY – THE ROOT OF ALL EVIL

If you grew up poor, then you have very likely brought some myths about money into your journey. Money affects us on an emotional level because it is a medium of exchange. It dictates the amount of our food, the size of our homes, the quality of our clothing, the nature of our vacations.

If you grew up without a lot of money, you can compare yourself to others who seem to have a lot of it. You look at their homes, their clothing and their meals. Ugly attitudes can begin to broil beneath the surface - envy, resentment, self-pity and bitterness. To cope with your insecurity you develop mythologies.

- People with a lot of money are miserable.
- People with a lot of money had opportunities I will never have.
- People with a lot of money are lucky stiffs who just happened to be in the right place at the right time.
- People with a lot of money are generally corrupt.
- People with a lot of money are shallow.
- People with a lot of money are selfish.

These mythologies sabotage you.

- If you experience failure in reaching your income goals, to ease the pain you go back to that old bitter resentment about 'people with money'.

OR

- If you actually start making money, you feel dirty about it. "Hey, look at you. You are becoming one of those evil people with a lot of money."

> *A goal statement is like oxygen. When you are being smothered by self-doubt and self-sabotaging thoughts, you need to pull out your goal statement and read it.*

Self-sabotaging thought: I'll SHOW YOU.

Sometimes our insecurities cause us to overcompensate, by setting our expectations too high. It can look like this.

You read about someone that started a company and became a millionaire overnight. You compare yourself to them and feel like a loser by comparison. So you rev up your expectations with an 'I'll show you' vengeance. "I'm going to start a company and make sales calls 10 hours a day every day, until I surpass you."

When you demand instant results, you set yourself up for failure. The initial voice of I am strong and competent will eventually be whittled down to a whimper of "I suck. I really do." Until you land at 'Oh, screw it. I give up."

THE CURE FOR SELF-SABOTAGE

Now that you know what to beware of, let's explore some ways that you can defeat the unhealthy thought process.

Read your goal statement

A goal statement is like oxygen. When you are being smothered by self-doubt and self-sabotaging thoughts, you need to pull out your goal statement and read it. It will breathe life back into your commitment to becoming the person you want to become, so you can live the life you want to live.

Get back on track

This guide was designed as a map from where you are to where you want to be. Revisit the steps that have been outlined in the guide and pick up where you left off. As you take action it will distance you from those self-sabotaging voices.

Step up your commitment to positive affirmation

You may have heard the Native American story of the two dogs. *"Inside of me there are two dogs. One of the dogs is mean and evil. The other dog is good. The mean dog fights the good dog, all of the time."* When asked which dog wins, the narrator reflected for a moment and replied, *"The one I feed the most."*

The same can be said of the good thoughts and bad thoughts barking in your head. The one you feed wins. Feed your attitude with positive affirmation and you will drown out the self-sabotaging thoughts.

Listen to audios

One of the most powerful tools for managing your negative thoughts and emotions is listening to motivational audios. Audios serve two purposes: They drown out the negative conversation going on in your head. More importantly, they inspire you with ideas on how live a life of purpose and achievement.

Align yourself with healthy individuals

Befriend someone who, like you, is committed to designing a life that they can love. Identify community groups that attract people 'on the move' and move forward with them.

You can find these purpose-driven people at business-oriented functions and community events. Learn to network. Dress appropriately, stoke your attitude with a motivational audio on the way, Stand tall, walk through the door and meet some people.

Getting 'on with your life' means letting go of the chains of the past. It doesn't mean rejecting others who feel no need to change. It means inspiring them with the hope that change is possible.

Man cannot discover new oceans
unless he has the courage to lose sight of the shore.

Andre Gide, Noble Prize winning author

Jesse Pipes

Director of World Camp for Kids,
Competitive Cyclist

It was the summer of 2000, my junior year at UNC – Chapel Hill. I had just turned 21. I can still picture our living room and the fake leather couch on Rosemary Street. It was there, on that couch that my two best friends and I first discussed starting an international non-profit organization dedicated to preventing the spread of AIDS.

significant. We wanted to do more than advocate from afar. We wanted to go into the communities afflicted by the AIDS pandemic and empower those at the grass roots to do what they needed to do to reverse this tragic disease trend.

This was a pretty big problem for 3 college kids, barely out of adolescents, to even consider tackling. But our passion to make a difference was bigger than the obstacles we were bound to face. We went for it, and formed our non-profit.

We were young, and certainly did not have the experience to qualify us to do such a thing. We had not studied public health or international development. We didn't have advanced degrees, or other qualifications.

What we did have was passion. Our passion was awakened by the knowledge of the devastating effect of the AIDS pandemic on children around the world. This disease kills parents and creates orphans. Such children face grave risks to their education, health, and well-being. They often suffer from anxiety, depression and abuse. Almost as lethal as the virus, is the stigma associated with the disease. Fear of being stigmatized creates a barrier to testing, treatment and prevention. This explains in part why many who are HIV-positive don't even know their status.

We were stirred to do something

World Camp for Kids was founded in 2000. In 2001, the original World Camp team traveled through southern Africa in a Volkswagen mini-bus living in tents. We were there to test our newly developed AIDS education curriculum in 21 primary schools. While there we witnessed the devastation of AIDS, firsthand. Seeing the problem up close fueled our passion and solidified our commitment to expand our effort.

Since 2000, we have raised up 500 dedicated volunteers who have helped us establish World Camp programs in Africa, Central America and India. Through our volunteers we have provided food, support and education to thousands of children, families and communities.

The World Camp story is evidence that age and experience do not matter. Your willingness to do what it takes to achieve your goals is what matters. Success is not about what your current resume claims you are capable of doing. It is about identifying a need and doing what you can to meet that need.

Some advice I would give to those with lofty goals: Decide what you want and go for it. Once you have decided, seize the moment and look for opportunities that will move you toward your goal.

Be sure to count the cost. Success comes with a price. Sometimes we see what other people have achieved and think it looks so easy. The truth is this – success in any venture requires careful planning, focused effort, persistence and patience.

Don't be intimidated by your lack of experience. You don't have to be an expert, before you launch your dream. You don't have to know everything at the beginning of your journey. You will learn much along the way. Your personality, intelligence, knowledge or talents are not static. As you challenge yourself, you will grow.

Don't forget to take time for yourself. It would be easy to fall into the trap of working all the time. Despite the demands of international travel and my workload I have learned to pursue other interests that sharpen me both physically and mentally. In addition to my work as Director of World Camp, I also enjoy competitive cycling.

Learn to appreciate the journey as much as the destination.

Shannon Wallace, Jr.

Founder of 386 Athletics

I grew up in Newport News, VA in a single family home. We had little money, but we had a lot of love. My early years were challenging. As a child, I was constantly sick. Another challenge was that crime and poverty were all around me. When you are surrounded by negativity, you are at risk of being swallowed up by it. Fortunately, I felt compelled to rise above the mediocrity around me and help others to do the same.

I overcame my childhood sickliness by getting involved in sports. I was committed to excelling at sports. I also realized that if I was going to rise above the poverty around me, I needed to do well in school. My commitment to both sports and academic achievement led to a scholarship to play college football.

Though my passion was sports and fitness, I chose to study finance and marketing. After all, if I was going to be a true success story, I needed to be wealthy. Successful people made lots of money, right? So making money became my goal.

After college I embarked on a career in sales, finance and marketing. In my early 20's, I was making good money through real estate investments. I also landed an excellent job with a Fortune 500 company. My competitive instincts served me well. I was skilled and persistent at chasing the next deal, choosing the right prospect, making even more money.

Surely, this must be the right path. After all, not only had I escaped a life of crime and mediocrity, I was getting rich. The problem was this. It felt wrong. I had fallen in love with my bank account, but I did not even like myself.

After 10+ years of grinding it out in the corporate world, I knew that I had to make a change. Mahatma Gandhi said it best by saying, *"Be the change you wish to see in the world."* I was ready for the next phase of my life.

I thought back to my days in sports. I loved football, martial arts and being fit. I began investigating various health and wellness careers. I studied reflexology, personal training, and even worked at a local vitamin store.

Everyone that knew me could not believe I had decided to leave the corporate world. I lost 'friends', lots of them. When people can make money off of you or can gain something from you, you have a lot of friends. When you no longer have anything to offer them, it is amazing how fast they disappear.

My passion to get involved in the health and wellness industry continued to grow. I knew that this was the right path for me; but I was not exactly certain where it would lead. I was walking by faith.

To stay motivated I read a lot. I listened to DVD's, attended workshops and obtained certifications. This kept me motivated.

I started journaling ideas as they came to me. When you write things down, you see things more clearly. You begin to formulate a vision for the future.

I traveled across the country to hear professional athletes and fitness specialists speak. I watched pro athletes train. My confidence increased. I knew I was headed in the right direction.

I was not making much money during this period, but I was enjoying the journey. I loved what I was learning and doing. It did not feel like work. I was pursuing my passion rather than my pension. I use to think that those who said such things were just making excuses for their laziness. I was totally wrong. When you are fulfilling your purpose you are successful, no matter what you bank account indicates.

It was during this time of soul searching and investigating my options that my philosophy of fitness began to form. I developed a concept I call the optimal fitness lifestyle. I designed a system that integrated all the modalities that lead to both wellness and fitness. My long journey, a journey that included many days of doubt and fear, culminated in the creation of 368 Athletics - a fitness system that encompasses what I consider to be the best of all the philosophies and systems I studied during my years of investigation.

368 Athletics reflects who I am - that kid from Newport News, VA who was determined to rise above mediocrity and help others do the same. I am doing what I was designed to do.

If you feel conflicted about the direction you need to take in life, here is a key: match your outer self to your inner self. If you do this you will never have to lie to yourself. Who I am as a person and how I will live the rest of my life can be summed up in the words of Ralph Waldo Emerson:

"To laugh often and much, to win the respect of intelligent people and the affection of honest critics and endure the betrayal of false friends, to appreciate beauty, to find the best in others, to leave the world a bit better, whether by a healthy child or a garden patch...to know even one life has breathed easier because you have lived, this is to have succeeded."

PART 5

Coach Lydia's 30 Day No-Nonsense Action Plan

**A JOURNEY OF A THOUSAND MILES
BEGINS WITH ONE STEP.**

By now, you are identifying steps you need to take to accomplish
what you want to accomplish in life. It is really important that you do not allow yourself to get uptight and blow a fuse. "Oh, my gosh. I have so much to do. Where do I begin?"

If you are feeling overwhelmed, I want you to stop, take a deep breath and let your mind clear. Remember back to those simple principles reinforced throughout this guide.

- Your journey toward your goals is accomplished one step at a time.
- Every step that you take toward your goals is a step in the right direction.
- Aim for progression not perfection.

To reinforce this principle in your life, grease the wheels of progress with a simple daily commitment. For the next 30 days, I want you to do 3 things that move you in the direction of your goal to GET OFF YOUR BUTT, OUT OF YOUR RUT, AND ON WITH YOUR LIFE.

Just 3 things!

IN THE MORNING BEFORE YOU START YOUR DAY:

Take a few minutes to read and/or pray about your daily quote.
Then write down 3 steps that will lead you toward the life you want to lead.

Example: Day 1:

1. Drink 2 quarts of water.
2. Call and resign from that committee that I volunteered for just to make my best friend happy, but it's making me miserable.
3. Commit 45 minutes to do Step 1 GET ON WITH YOUR LIFE
   [Contemplate the Past.]

AT THE END OF THE DAY, ASK YOURSELF A SIMPLE QUESTION.

Did I do what I committed to do?

The answer to that simple question is equally simple.

Yes? or No?

If you don't accomplish all 3 things due to circumstances beyond control, just transfer the items you missed to the next day. I don't consider things like – I forgot or I just didn't get around to it - to be circumstances beyond your control. Those are excuses, not reasons.

You are in the driver's seat. You decide what you want to accomplish. It's your choice. But something amazing and life-changing will happen if you commit to this simple plan. I guarantee it – 100%. You want to know what it is?

At the end of 30 days you will be closer to your goals!

Another amazing thing will happen.

You will be skilled at mentally preparing [Reading your quote.] and setting your goals, taking action [3 simple steps a day!] and monitoring your progress [Yes, I did or No, I did not do what I committed to do].

Just like learning to ride a bike, once you have learned a couple basics – how to balance and press the pedals – you can take off the training wheels. Before long you will be ditching the bike and mounting a Harley.

We all start somewhere.

For some of you this pace will be too slow. You are ready to establish 1 year, 5 year and 10 year goals and develop the action plan for reaching them. That's great! I certainly do not want to slow you down. Go for it!

But for those of you who do not know where to begin. Start here.

Every step that you take toward your goals is a step in the right direction.

I would encourage you to seek out like-minded friends who can hold you accountable. There are others like you who are being inspired to start living a life of purpose; others, like you, who are ready to get off their butt, out of their rut and on with their lives. Start or join an accountability group. For ideas on how to begin an accountability group visit www.alifenow.com.

If you need the assistance of a wellness or life coach to keep you on track during the process of change, find one. Consider it an investment in yourself – one of the most important investments you can make.

Day 1

*It was character that got us out of bed,
commitment that moved us into action,
and discipline that enabled us to follow through.*

Zig Ziglar

**TODAY (_____)
I WILL DO AT LEAST THREE THINGS
THAT LEAD ME TOWARD MY GOAL OF GETTING**
Off my Butt
Out of my Rut
On with my Life

☐ **1.**

☐ **2.**

☐ **3.**

Day 2

You don't have to be great to get started,
but you have to get started to be great.

Les Brown

TODAY (_____)
I WILL DO AT LEAST THREE THINGS
THAT LEAD ME TOWARD MY GOAL OF GETTING

Off my Butt
Out of my Rut
On with my Life

☐ 1.

☐ 2.

☐ 3.

Day 3

*The two important things I did learn were that
you are as powerful and strong as you allow yourself to be,
and that the most difficult part of any endeavor
is taking the first step, making the first decision.*

Robyn Davidson

TODAY (_____)
I WILL DO AT LEAST THREE THINGS
THAT LEAD ME TOWARD MY GOAL OF GETTING
Off my Butt
Out of my Rut
On with my Life

☐ 1.

☐ 2.

☐ 3.

Day 4

You are responsible for your life.
You can't keep blaming somebody else for your dysfunction.
Life is really about moving on.

Oprah Winfrey

TODAY (_____)
I WILL DO AT LEAST THREE THINGS
THAT LEAD ME TOWARD MY GOAL OF GETTING

Off my Butt

Out of my Rut

On with my Life

☐ **1.**

☐ **2.**

☐ **3.**

Day 5

It is for us to pray not for tasks equal to our powers,
but for powers equal to our tasks;
To go forward with a great desire
forever beating at the door of our hearts
as we travel toward our distant goal.

Helen Keller

TODAY (_____)
I WILL DO AT LEAST THREE THINGS
THAT LEAD ME TOWARD MY GOAL OF GETTING
Off my Butt
Out of my Rut
On with my Life

☐ **1.**

☐ **2.**

☐ **3.**

Day 6

There are many ways of going forward,
but only one way of standing still.

Franklin D. Roosevelt

TODAY (_____)
I WILL DO AT LEAST THREE THINGS
THAT LEAD ME TOWARD MY GOAL OF GETTING

Off my Butt
Out of my Rut
On with my Life

☐ **1.**

☐ **2.**

☐ **3.**

Day 7

Don't let the past steal your present.

Terri Guillemets

TODAY (_____)
I WILL DO AT LEAST THREE THINGS
THAT LEAD ME TOWARD MY GOAL OF GETTING
Off my Butt
Out of my Rut
On with my Life

☐ **1.**

☐ **2.**

☐ **3.**

Day 8

If you are still talking about what you did yesterday,
you haven't done much today.

Author Unknown

TODAY (_____)
I WILL DO AT LEAST THREE THINGS
THAT LEAD ME TOWARD MY GOAL OF GETTING

Off my Butt
Out of my Rut
On with my Life

☐ **1.**

☐ **2.**

☐ **3.**

Day 9

When one door closes, another door opens;
but we so often look so long and so regretfully upon the closed door,
that we do not see the ones which open for us.

Alexander Graham Bell

TODAY (_____)
I WILL DO AT LEAST THREE THINGS
THAT LEAD ME TOWARD MY GOAL OF GETTING

Off my Butt
Out of my Rut
On with my Life

☐ 1.

☐ 2.

☐ 3.

Day 10

Develop an attitude of gratitude, and give thanks for everything that happens to you, knowing that every step forward is a step toward achieving something bigger and better than your current situation.

Brian Tracy

TODAY (_____)
I WILL DO AT LEAST THREE THINGS
THAT LEAD ME TOWARD MY GOAL OF GETTING

Off my Butt

Out of my Rut

On with my Life

☐ **1.**

☐ **2.**

☐ **3.**

Day 11

Do you want to know who you are?
Don't ask. Act!
Action will delineate and define you.

Thomas Jefferson

TODAY (_____)
I WILL DO AT LEAST THREE THINGS
THAT LEAD ME TOWARD MY GOAL OF GETTING

Off my Butt

Out of my Rut

On with my Life

☐ 1.

☐ 2.

☐ 3.

Day 12

*Remember, a real decision is measured by the fact
that you've taken new action.
If there's no action, you haven't truly decided.*

Tony Robbins

TODAY (_____)
I WILL DO AT LEAST THREE THINGS
THAT LEAD ME TOWARD MY GOAL OF GETTING

Off my Butt

Out of my Rut

On with my Life

☐ **1.**

☐ **2.**

☐ **3.**

Day 13

Action is a great restorer and builder of confidence.
Inaction is not only the result, but the cause, of fear.
Perhaps the action you take will be successful;
perhaps different action or adjustments will have to follow.
But any action is better than no action at all.

Norman Vincent Peale

TODAY (_____)
I WILL DO AT LEAST THREE THINGS
THAT LEAD ME TOWARD MY GOAL OF GETTING

Off my Butt
Out of my Rut
On with my Life

☐ **1.**

☐ **2.**

☐ **3.**

Day 14

Watch your thoughts, for they become words.
Watch your words, for they become actions.
Watch your actions, for they become habits.
Watch your habits, for they become character.
Watch your character, for it becomes your destiny.

Unknown

TODAY (_____)
I WILL DO AT LEAST THREE THINGS
THAT LEAD ME TOWARD MY GOAL OF GETTING

Off my Butt

Out of my Rut

On with my Life

☐ **1.**

☐ **2.**

☐ **3.**

Day 15

There's a difference between interest and commitment.
When you're interested in doing something,
you do it only when circumstance permit.
When you're committed to something,
you accept no excuses, only results.

Unknown

TODAY (_____)
I WILL DO AT LEAST THREE THINGS
THAT LEAD ME TOWARD MY GOAL OF GETTING

Off my Butt

Out of my Rut

On with my Life

☐ **1.**

☐ **2.**

☐ **3.**

Day 16

To increase your effectiveness,
make your emotions subordinate to you commitments.

Brian Koslow

TODAY (_____)
I WILL DO AT LEAST THREE THINGS
THAT LEAD ME TOWARD MY GOAL OF GETTING
Off my Butt
Out of my Rut
On with my Life

☐ **1.**

☐ **2.**

☐ **3.**

Day 17

We must all suffer from one of two pains:
the pain of discipline or the pain of regret.
The difference is discipline weighs ounces while regret weighs tons.

Jim Rohn

TODAY (_____)
I WILL DO AT LEAST THREE THINGS
THAT LEAD ME TOWARD MY GOAL OF GETTING
Off my Butt
Out of my Rut
On with my Life

☐ **1.**

☐ **2.**

☐ **3.**

Day 18

*Discipline is based on pride, on meticulous attention to details,
and on mutual respect and confidence.
Discipline must be a habit so ingrained that it is stronger than the
excitement of the goal or the fear of failure.*

Gary Ryan Blair

TODAY (_____)
I WILL DO AT LEAST THREE THINGS
THAT LEAD ME TOWARD MY GOAL OF GETTING
Off my Butt
Out of my Rut
On with my Life

☐ 1.

☐ 2.

☐ 3.

Day 19

We are what we repeatedly do.
Excellence, then, is not an act, but a habit.

Aristotle

TODAY (_____)
I WILL DO AT LEAST THREE THINGS
THAT LEAD ME TOWARD MY GOAL OF GETTING

Off my Butt
Out of my Rut
On with my Life

☐ 1.

☐ 2.

☐ 3.

Day 20

No horse gets anywhere until he is harnessed.
No stream or gas drives anything until it is confined.
No Niagara is ever turned into light and power until it is tunneled.
No life ever grows great until it is focused, dedicated, disciplined.

Harry Emerson Fosdick

TODAY (_____)
I WILL DO AT LEAST THREE THINGS
THAT LEAD ME TOWARD MY GOAL OF GETTING

Off my Butt

Out of my Rut

On with my Life

☐ **1.**

☐ **2.**

☐ **3.**

Day 21

No one is in control of your happiness but you;
therefore, you have the power to change anything about yourself
or your life that you want to change.

Barbara de Angelis

TODAY (_____)
I WILL DO AT LEAST THREE THINGS
THAT LEAD ME TOWARD MY GOAL OF GETTING
Off my Butt
Out of my Rut
On with my Life

☐ **1.**

☐ **2.**

☐ **3.**

Day 22

I cannot believe that the purpose of life is to be "happy."
I think the purpose of life is to be useful, to be responsible,
to be compassionate.
It is, above all, to matter and to count,
to stand for something,
to have made some difference that you lived at all.

Leo C. Rosten

TODAY (_____)
I WILL DO AT LEAST THREE THINGS
THAT LEAD ME TOWARD MY GOAL OF GETTING

Off my Butt

Out of my Rut

On with my Life

☐ **1.**

☐ **2.**

☐ **3.**

Day 23

Don't rely on someone else for your happiness and self worth.
Only you can be responsible for that.
If you can't love and respect yourself,
-no one else will be able to make that happen.
Accept who you are - completely;
the good and the bad - and make changes as YOU see fit –
not because you think someone else wants you to be different.

Stacey Charter

TODAY (_____)
I WILL DO AT LEAST THREE THINGS
THAT LEAD ME TOWARD MY GOAL OF GETTING

Off my Butt

Out of my Rut

On with my Life

☐ 1.

☐ 2.

☐ 3.

Day 24

Courage doesn't always roar.
Sometimes courage is the quiet voice at the end of the day saying,
"I will try again tomorrow."

Mary Anne Radmacher

TODAY (_____)
I WILL DO AT LEAST THREE THINGS
THAT LEAD ME TOWARD MY GOAL OF GETTING

Off my Butt

Out of my Rut

On with my Life

☐ **1.**

☐ **2.**

☐ **3.**

Day 25

Life is like riding a bicycle.
To keep your balance you must keep moving.

Albert Einstein

TODAY (_____)
I WILL DO AT LEAST THREE THINGS
THAT LEAD ME TOWARD MY GOAL OF GETTING

Off my Butt
Out of my Rut
On with my Life

☐ **1.**

☐ **2.**

☐ **3.**

Day 26

People can be more forgiving than you can imagine.
But you have to forgive yourself.
Let go of what's bitter and move on.

Bill Cosby

TODAY (_____)
I WILL DO AT LEAST THREE THINGS
THAT LEAD ME TOWARD MY GOAL OF GETTING

Off my Butt

Out of my Rut

On with my Life

☐ **1.**

☐ **2.**

☐ **3.**

Day 27

The truth is that our finest moments are most likely to occur when we are feeling deeply uncomfortable, unhappy, or unfulfilled.

For it is only in such moments, propelled by our discomfort, that we are likely to step out of our ruts and start searching for different ways or truer answers.

M. Scott Peck

TODAY (_____)
I WILL DO AT LEAST THREE THINGS
THAT LEAD ME TOWARD MY GOAL OF GETTING
Off my Butt
Out of my Rut
On with my Life

☐ **1.**

☐ **2.**

☐ **3.**

Day 28

*The path of least resistance and least trouble
is a mental rut already made.*

*It requires troublesome work to undertake the alternation
of old beliefs.*

John Dewey

TODAY (_____)
I WILL DO AT LEAST THREE THINGS
THAT LEAD ME TOWARD MY GOAL OF GETTING

Off my Butt

Out of my Rut

On with my Life

☐ **1.**

☐ **2.**

☐ **3.**

Day 29

What is not started today is never finished tomorrow.

Johann Wolfgang

TODAY (_____)
I WILL DO AT LEAST THREE THINGS
THAT LEAD ME TOWARD MY GOAL OF GETTING
Off my Butt
Out of my Rut
On with my Life

☐ 1.

☐ 2.

☐ 3.

Day 30

You are never too old to set another goal or to dream a new dream.

C.S. Lewis

TODAY (_____)
I WILL DO AT LEAST THREE THINGS
THAT LEAD ME TOWARD MY GOAL OF GETTING

Off my Butt

Out of my Rut

On with my Life

☐ **1.**

☐ **2.**

☐ **3.**

NOW WHAT?

That is a great question that only you can answer.

Hate to break the news, but this is the truth. God doesn't hand you a tight schedule for every moment of your life so you don't have to think.

What you are given is:

- Time as your starting block and finish line
- Food as your fuel
- Wisdom as your guide and
- Talent as your tools.

It's up to you on how you use that time, choose that food, apply that wisdom and use those tools.

You decide.

Your life will be the outcome of those decisions. That can be a scary thought, but remember - there is grace in the journey.

Don't be paralyzed by the fear of making the wrong decision. Life is not figured out in a moment. It is a process of trial and error. Starting down one path does not mean that the door to other paths will close. You can and should adjust your course along the way.

Now what? is the question you will be asking yourself each step of your journey. The only thing that can stop your progress toward your goals is if you stop thinking about the answer.

For resources to help you answer that question visit

www.lydiamartinez.com

There you will find educational and organization tools,

Bonnie Church's life-coaching blog and other valuable links to help you

get [and stay!] off your butt, out of your rut and on with your life.

COACH LYDIA MARTINEZ

"If you are not willing to risk the unusual, you will have to settle for the ordinary." Jim Rohn

Lydia Martinez transforms the lives of everyday people - physically, mentally and emotionally. She has coached thousands of people to take control of their life and lose weight, body fat, and inches through proven systems.

Lydia has seen far too many loved ones die far too young from diet and lifestyle related disease. This has fueled her commitment to ongoing health, nutrition and fitness education. She is a CPT, NESTA Child Nutrition Specialist, and Certified Under Armor Combine 360 Trainer.

She is a sought after seminar speaker and coach. Not one to be restrained, Lydia's optimism, humor, honesty and passion for life motivates others to look better, feel better, have more energy, and take up less room. Her own personal journey from hardship to success enables her to relate to people from all demographics: children, adults, rich and poor, well-educated and under educated.

Lydia currently serves as the Director of a multimillion-dollar lifestyle weight loss program. She is creative director of the number one child and family lifestyle program in the United States. She is changing the future of our children's health one family at a time.

BONNIE CHURCH

Bonnie Church is a writer and a practicing life and wellness coach. She is also a Certified Transitions Lifestyle coach, certified nutritional consultant and certified life coach. She has helped hundreds, directly or indirectly, reach their life and wellness goals. Bonnie is a popular motivational speaker who has entertained and encouraged nationwide audiences. Her professional writing career spans 25 years. She has served as a columnist, journalist, content editor and ghost writer for internationally known authors. She has co-authored training and coaching materials to support life and wellness-related programs. Bonnie is currently the Healthy Lady Columnist for *All About Women Magazine*. You can read her life-coaching blog at http://www.alifenow.com

Recommended Resources

NUTRITION

Websites:
www.lydiamartinez.com
www.transitionslifestylesystem.com
www.glycemicindex.com

Books:
Prescription for Nutritional Healing Phyllis A. Balch, CNC
The Complete Idiots Guide to Glycemic Index Weight Loss Beale and Warner
The Everything Glycemic Index Cookbook Nancy T. Maar

Products:

General Health:
Isotonix™: Multivitamin, B-Complex, OPC3 and Calcium (Market America)
NutriClean® HepatoCleanse Liver Support Formula (Market America)
NutriClean® Probiotics (Market America)
Heart Health ™ Omega III

Adrenal Support:
TLS™ ACTS Adrenal, Cortisol, Thyroid and Stress Support Formula
(Market America)
End Fatigue Daily Energy Enfusion™ (Integrative Therapeutics)
Isocort™ (Bezwecken)
Seriphos® Phoshorylated Serin (interPlexus,Inc)

Weight Loss
Transitions Lifestyle System Journal
TLS™ CORE Fat and Carb Inhibitor (Market America)
TLS™ CLA Conjugated Linoleic Acid (Market America)
TLS™ "On the Go" Shakes

FITNESS

Websites:
www.lydiamartinez.com
www.368athletics.com
www.exercise.com
www.combine360.com

Books:
Transitions Lifestyle Journal Market America
The IMPACT Body Plan Todd Durken
5-Factor Fitness Harley Pasternak

PERSONAL CARE

Skincare:
Pumice Cleanser (Derma)
Cellular Laboratories® De-Aging Eye Crème (Market America)
Matriskin™ Collagen MP Serum (Market America)
Cellular Laboratories® De-Aging Créme (Market America)
Cellular Laboratories® De-Aging Day Creme SPF 20 (Market America)

Make up:
Motives by Loren Ridinger – high quality, fairly priced, customizable cosmetics

FASHION:

Websites:
www.myfashioncents.com
www.lorensworld.com

LEADERSHIP and PERSONAL GROWTH

Websites:
www.lydiamartinez.com
www.alifenow.com
www.danijohnson.com
www.johnmaxwell.com
www.successmagazine.com
www.beingjrridinger.com

Books:
The Difference Maker John C. Maxwell
The 21 Irrefutable Laws of Leadership John C. Maxwell
The 360 Degree Leader John C. Maxwell
Moral Earthquakes and Secret Faults O.S. Hawkins
Reposition Yourself T.D. Jakes
The Four Agreements: A Practical Guide to Personal Freedom Don Miguel Ruiz

The Dream Giver Bruce Wilkinson
The Rhythm of Life   Matthew Kelly
When God Whispers Your Name   Max Lucado
Life Wisdom from Coach Wooden   John Wooden
Communication and the Art of Persuasion Jim Rohn
Living an Exceptional Life Jim Rohn
The Richest Man in Babylon George S. Clason

MONEY MANAGEMENT

Money management system: MaCapital Resources
www.macapitalresources.com

Books:
Spirit Driven Success Dani Johnson
Women & Money: Owning the Power to Control Your Destiny Suzie Orman
The Total Money Makeover Dave Ramsey